Too few apples:

The challenge
of declining enrolments
and teacher redundancy
in Canada

Richard J. Chamberlin

The Canadian Education Association
1980 $5

About the author

Richard Chamberlin obtained his B.A. (Hons.) in Economics from the University of Winnipeg and his M.A. in the same subject from the University of Manitoba. He has worked as a policy analyst and researcher for the Manitoba and British Columbia governments, and was director of research with the Alberta Department of Consumer and Corporate Affairs for four years. After a year as a reporter and feature writer with the *Edmonton Journal,* Mr. Chamberlin moved to Winnipeg in 1979 to take up freelance writing full-time. He is currently working on projects in Canadian history, consumerism, and education.

© The Canadian Education Association 1980

ISBN 0-919078-64-8

Produced in Canada by Drewmark Graphics
Cover design by William Soles & Associates

Foreword

In the fall of 1979 the Canadian Education Association commissioned Richard J. Chamberlin to prepare an English manuscript on teacher redundancy and retraining in Canada. At the same time CEA commissioned Guy Brouillet to prepare a French manuscript on the subject. Mr. Chamberlin and M. Brouillet were asked to attend the November 1979 CEA seminar on the topic, and then to conduct research across the country so that in-depth reports might be published.

The authors worked independently of each other and so the two booklets, both of which are now available from the CEA, (French title *Le temps du recyclage*) are different in approach and content, though both provide a wealth of information.

Two Few Apples: Meeting the Challenge of Declining Enrolments and Teacher Redundancy in Canada offers many positive suggestions for resolving the problems faced especially by teachers who find themselves declared redundant now, or who may face that situation in the near future. The author has gathered together practical ideas for teachers, faculties of education, ministries or departments of education, school boards and their officials.

Although any opinions expressed in this publication are those of the author and do not necessarily reflect the views of the Canadian Education Association, there is no doubt that this booklet can be of service to all those involved in education who are experiencing — or who are about to experience — the effects of declining enrolments.

Gerald Nason
Executive Director
Canadian Education Association

Contents

List of tables

Preface

There is by no means a consensus on teacher redundancy in Canada; views range from alarm to indifference. But the attendance of educators and administrators from every province at an Ottawa convention on redundancy last year belies the confidence some officials, unconcerned with excess teacher supply, have expressed. Redundancy may not be universal, but it remains a possibility for any school board. And, more important, the attention to sound school management which the redundancy scare has called forth appears to be a wise preoccupation for any administrator.

This monograph does not offer an exhaustive list of the elements of teacher demand and supply or a rigorous analysis of their interaction. Rather, the terms of reference for the project stressed a selective review of programs dealing with excess teacher supply, outlining their nature and success. It was thought such an overview would be of value in at least two ways. Jurisdictions experiencing enrolment declines, or some of the other sources of instability in the school system, and puzzling over remedies or taking action, would benefit. And school boards encountering few if any problems, but which nonetheless do not discount the chance of a disturbance in the future, should welcome a scanning of current activity in this field.

The concern of the study has been with the human side of contraction in the education sector, not with school facilities. The discussion therefore concentrates on means of alleviating excess teacher supply and excludes an analysis of capital resources. The statistics and factual content of the monograph are current to January, 1980, unless otherwise indicated; the reader is cautioned that more recent information may have come to light since.

I am deeply grateful to the following people for their assistance in the preparation of this report: Diane Sibbett, librarian, Canadian Education Association, Toronto; Robert S. Wyatt, colleague and friend; Geraldine Gilliss, director of research, Canadian Teachers' Federation, Ottawa; and the many teachers and administrators who spoke candidly of their problems.

Richard J. Chamberlin
Winnipeg, Manitoba
January 1980

Chapter 1
Introduction

Since her childhood, Wendy Green has wanted to teach. She would come home from school in her native Bathurst, New Brunswick, and stand at a makeshift blackboard in her basement where she would used coloured chalk to instruct her younger sisters in spelling and letters.

Wendy entered the University of New Brunswick, taking two years of arts, a year off, then four years of education, graduating in the spring of 1979 with a Certificate Four in Education and a specialty in secondary arts and English. She began looking for a job.

Seventy applications later, some to the Yukon and Northwest Territories, the good news came: there were openings in Bathurst, Chipman, and Perth-Andover. Interviews were held, but despite her excellent marks, Wendy was passed over for the positions. There were just too many others after the same jobs.

Wendy is substitute teaching these days in Bathurst, a role she approaches with mixed emotions. She's gaining actual classroom experience and getting to know the youngsters and the methods of the other teachers. But the stress is mounting. Being notified of the school she will teach at just an hour ahead of the first bell, not knowing the children's names, being taken for a pushover by classes disdainful of fill-in teachers, and earning less that she could full-time, are frustrating Wendy. She has applied for teacher certification in Alberta. If her crop of applications fails to locate something permanent, Wendy will head west.

It cost Wendy about $32,000 in foregone earnings to stay out of the job market and attend the faculty of education. And it cost the faculty and the people of New Brunswick another $14,000 or so to transform the dream of a child into a near reality. These sunk economic costs remain to be recouped by the young teacher and the taxpayers who helped finance her training. Substitute teaching is making only a dent in that debt. And if she leaves New Brunswick, the debt to the community can only be written off to experience.

Wendy Green's case in not unique. Throughout Canada, and particularly in larger urban centres, teacher graduates aren't finding work or are taking jobs unsuited to their training. In Winnipeg and Saskatoon, for example, scores of graduates didn't find teaching posts last fall. Many, of course, were simply unwilling to move to rural areas where teachers are still in demand; but others were unable to relocate.

Equally disheartening is the experience of many teachers who have planned their lives around a career in the classroom, only to find they're no longer needed. School boards in Ontario have fired teachers; boards in Montreal have placed hundreds on recall lists; and boards on the Prairies and in British Columbia fear they will have to let more teachers go. Many of the educators in question face not only an interruption of earnings, but the jolt of a career change if they wish to continue working and support their families.

The villain is vague and elusive, though its effects are clear: a mismatch of teacher supply and demand is at the root of the disturbance and it's shaking education to its foundations. Too many teachers are entering the profession or returning to it after a rest or a venture into another field; fewer teachers are retiring early or taking leave to raise families. Cutthroat competition for teaching posts is the result. Births and school enrolments are down, in some areas dramatically, so teaching jobs are fewer. Education has slipped as a government spending priority; the bankrolls of the 1960s and early 1970s are gone.

So education students are wondering if they made the right career choice. Teachers' morale is fading as they speculate on their job prospects, be they within or outside teaching. Administrators struggle to manage wisely a contracting school system, a task they're finding more difficult than guiding the growth that system once knew. And reliance on seniority as the arbiter of teacher employment during excess supply is contributing to the aging of the teacher force as it entrenches older teachers, dismisses younger ones, and bars graduates from the profession.

The social costs of training teachers, then failing to hire them, could be substantial. Four per cent of Canada's education class of 1976 were looking for work in 1978. Of those employed, fewer than three-quarters had found jobs as elementary or secondary educators. Though many of those not teaching are still able to apply the skills they've learned, the fact remains they're benefiting from only a portion of a costly education.

Steps taken to equalize teacher supply and demand have been numerous. In Southern Manitoba, a worried school board has asked adults to return to the classroom and continue their education at whatever level it ceased, hoping the increased enrolment will save jobs. In London, Ontario, teachers may take a year off "with pay", financing the leave through salary deductions in years prior to and following the absence. In Quebec, surplus teachers may retire a year early with full pay, provided the move opens a position for a teacher out of work.

But several obstacles are hindering these and other strategies. Concerned with economic instability, many teachers are averse to part-time and substitute teaching or early retirement, all of which mean lower earnings. The tenure system in Quebec, assuring teachers of permanent positions after two years of service, guarantees a salary to unneeded teachers and makes excess supply a particularly expensive problem. Fields of alternative education, among them adult basic education and kindergarten, could be expanded to absorb surplus teachers, yet remain largely ignored.

Finances pose a problem, too. Fewer and fewer voters have school-age children, and the average age of Canadians is rising. Spending on education is less likely to be important to these people and to the governments they elect. Shrinking education budgets, already in evidence, will make teacher training more difficult, the expansion of alternative education markets minimal, and lower pupil-teacher ratios improbable. The allocation of existing moneys within education has come under attack. Management claims that its allotment fails to meet the need imposed by the difficulty of managing contraction. And those teachers anxious to broaden their knowledge and strengthen their versatility find professional development spending insufficient.

Although some say excess teacher supply, or redundancy, will pass, there remains a pressing need for action, both in understanding the forces which brought redundancy into being, and in devising long-term strategies to avoid future upsets. In meeting these responsibilities, school boards face the challenge of presenting an image of thrift and accountability to a growingly critical electorate, weary of excesses of any kind.

Redundancy presents opportunities, too. Faced with a buyer's market for educators, school boards now have the chance to strengthen the quality of the teacher force. And, aware of excess capacity and excess staff in the school system advocates of adult basic and continuing education, of special education for children with special needs, and of pre-school education, now have a new premise in their argument for more resources.

Whether asset or liability, redundancy remains a condition which demands attention. And as the following chapters reveal, its causes are many, its effect profound, and its remedies diverse and sometimes elusive.

Chapter 2
Teacher redundancy: its causes and effects

The term redundancy means, simply, too many. Applied to prose, it denotes verbiage; to weaponry, proliferation. Applied to the teaching profession, it signifies an excessive number of educators, people no longer needed by their students. Yet, redundancy has been known to prevail amidst shortages of teacher manpower. The reasoning behind this apparent contradiction rests largely on semantics.

An overall glut of teachers means, of course, a clear case of redundancy. But there may, for example, be too many teachers in some subjects and too few in others. The fact it can take some years to retrain and reallocate such surplus instructors means in the short-run they're redundant. And there may, for example, be too many teachers in a particular school, a division, or a region of a province or a country. The fact that some of these teachers are unable or unwilling to move elsewhere to practise their calling means they too are redundant.

So the definition of the term depends on when it is used and on the willingness of administrators and planners to recognize as a fact of the labour market that education graduates want to work in their home towns.

However defined, redundancy is by no means a universal condition in Canada. But where it does prevail, it is a serious condition. And where it hasn't struck, it is often the subject of discussion and concern. The worry redundancy provokes is rooted in its multitude of causes, with no single force claiming the credit for eroding teacher security and school board control.

The causes

Excess teachers are a symptom of mismatched supply and demand. Thus, redundancy has its origins in those factors responsible for the level of the need for teachers, on the one hand, and their availability, on the other. Enrolments, pupil-teacher ratios, changes in teachers' service obligations or in pupils' timetables, and opportunities for in-service training, are the prominent ingredients on the demand side of the equation. On the supply side, the teachers from last year returning to teach in the current year, departures and re-entries since last year, and new entrants, are the principal determinants of the teacher stock in the current year. Each figures in the teacher market and each can bear on the extent of redundancy. While it is not entirely clear what factors *have caused* excess supply, there is a variety of market forces which *can cause* it.

Enrolments Between 1972 and 1978, Ontario's elementary and Roman Catholic separate schools lost 145,168 students, more than twice the decrease expected from 1972 to 1990. The final report of that province's Commission on Declining Enrolments (CODE) predicts an enrolment drop of 55 per cent in some areas. Prince Edward Island's Unit Two school board registered an enrolment decline of 200 students in October 1978, and expects to lose 1,000 pupils and 50 teachers over the next four years. From 1971 to 1976, Manitoba's enrolments declined by about 7 per cent. In British Columbia, elementary school students were 1.6 per cent fewer and secondary enrolments 2.3 per cent less in 1978 than in 1977.

In Canada, enrolments in kindergarten and elementary schools should fall from 4 million in 1972 to 3.32 million in 1981, then rise to 3.67 million by 1990. Secondary school enrolments, which reached their peak of 1.83 million in 1975, fell slowly to 1.77 million in 1978, then should move quickly to 1.44 million in 1983, and slowly to 1.34 million in 1990. Total secondary enrolments should fall by a half million in 14 years, a drop of 27 per cent.[1]

---

[1] Organisation for Economic Co-operation and Development, *Teacher Policies in a New Context* (1979), p. 41.

Still, 25 per cent of Canadian school boards recorded enrolment increases from 1976 to 1977. A further 11 per cent faced drops of less than 1 per cent. According to Table 1, below, which compares changes in school board enrolments from 1973-77 with those from 1976-77, there was a shift in emphasis in the more recent period.

Over the entire four years the bulk of enrolment declines amounted to between 7 to 19 per cent, but in the final year of that period, the majority of losses were less than 7 per cent, and may were less than 1 per cent. These statistics suggest that although enrolments are falling, the drop has not been precipitous in many jurisdictions.

School enrolments depend not only on births, but on the rate at which students pass or repeat grades and on the drop-out rate of secondary students. For Canada overall, the success rate for pupils in the secondary grades is estimated at just less than 90 per cent. So, secondary classes will be smaller than they might have been, quite apart from the birth rate or other demographic factors. The enrolment rate, comprising both the rate at which students enter schools, and the rate of their progression through the grades, can reflect the response of parents and youngsters to educational opportunities. A low enrolment can follow from economic difficulties — the direct

Table 1

Numbers of school boards encountering enrolment changes, 1973-1977, Canada

Percentage change in enrolment	1973-1977		1976-1977	
	Boards encountering increase	Boards encountering decrease	Boards encountering increase	Boards encountering decrease
Less than 1%	16	20	49	101
1 to 7%	109	141	128	469
7 to 13%	40	207	27	77
13 to 19%	20	145	7	9
19 to 25%	14	73	7	4
More than 25%	38	42	5	3
Total*	**237**	**628**	**223**	**663**

*Totals from 1976-77 are greater than 1973-77 because some school boards separated over the period in question.
Source: C.T. Curteis, Education, Science, and Culture Division, Statistics Canada, Ottawa. Unpublished paper (November 1979).

costs of schooling as well as the indirect costs of lost earnings while at school, cultural and language barriers, and difficulty of physical access to schools. Other things equal, the lower the enrolment, the less the demand for teachers.

The pupil-teacher ratio The pupil-teacher ratio, a formula deciding the number of teachers needed, is the result of choices in several areas of school and curriculum organization. These include: what is to be taught and learned; the teaching method to be employed; and average class size, number of teacher contact periods required by a class over a complete teaching cycle, and teaching load per teacher.

The content of learning — the curriculum — sets a pattern of experiences for the pupil; this will carry implications for the use of teachers. Teaching methods may involve more or less teacher-student interaction and, therefore, more or fewer teachers. Such pedagogical techniques may stress lecture, self-study with or without supervision, use of radio or television, group or individual tutorials, and so on. Each will alter the demand for teachers. Given pedagogical method and curriculum content, average class size will be greater or less, depending on size and number of classrooms. In rural areas, population distribution may constrain class size — countries with large and scattered rural populations will almost always have pupil-teacher ratios below the norm. The amount of teacher contact time required by a class will be greater if the class is subdivided for discussion or remedial work; this will tend to boost teacher demand. But the occurrence of self-study periods or of combined classes for films, lectures, or games, will save on teacher time. Finally, the average number of contact periods each teacher is expected to manage — a per person teaching load — will fall where junior teachers dominate or where several staff members have administrative posts.

Changes in service obligations Although of minor impact on teacher demand, this influence can occur where schools are experiencing the special problems associated with their location in urban cores or with a high proportion of immigrants' children. Often, these institutions will receive additional resources enabling them to acquire more staff of varying types, including teachers. So, the demand for teachers can rise in response to this impetus, working to the favour of the redundant teacher. Any new emphasis on a particular subject area will also trigger an effect on demand. For example, the growth of career counselling in schools, or the concern with second languages, will signal a need for instructors in these areas. Budgets permitting, this need will translate into a greater demand for teachers. However, teacher requirement will fall and redundancy will intensify where courses shrink in importance.

The stock of teachers The stock of teachers consists of teachers serving in schools plus those on temporary leave. Schools can be staffed beyond their needs or they can be short-staffed — the fact teachers are employed does not necessarily mean they're needed. The teacher stock in any one year is composed of those educators carried over from the previous year, but it is still subject to deterioration and loss. Teachers die, fall ill, and retire. They take extended leaves or resign. As well, the stock is subject to replenishment. Teachers re-enter the profession and they enter it anew. The stock has been rising recently as fewer teachers leave and more enter.

Departures Departures due to death and retirement are easily forecast, determined by the age distribution of people already born. Departures for other reasons, among them moves to other occupations, refusal to move to find a teaching post, maternity and educational leave, are more difficult to predict because they depend on social conditions, the health of the economy, and the opportunity for professional development. And because departures may vary markedly from one year to the next, their impact on teacher supply can be rapid and unpredictable. Fewer departures will accentuate redundancy.

Canada's elementary school teacher departure rate, about 10 per cent in 1974, is expected to fall to 7.5 per cent by 1990, slightly higher than the unchanging 5 per cent figure for secondary teachers[2]. Fewer departures at the elementary level reflect fewer teachers leaving to enrol in higher education or to manage households. In Ontario, for example, between 1965 and 1970, about a third of all elementary teacher force resignations were due to "married women retiring to household".[3]

Terminations depend on many factors, including working conditions in education compared with other professions; the chance for promotion; that professional support so important in an isolated job where morale depends on the leadership qualities of supervisors; and the degree of fairness in the personnel administration function.

Re-entry and new entry While re-entry is a supply factor

[2] *Ibid.*

[3] Peter Williams, *Planning Teacher Demand and Supply* (1979), p. 55.

difficult to predict, it is at the same time easier to influence than departures, thus offering the planner a ready source of recruitment, helping him to adjust supply to demand. Depending as it does on alternative job opportunities, re-entry will be greater in times of economic slack. If the downward trend of departure rates continues, it could be possible to meet the demand for teachers through re-entry. However, new entrants create a balance of ages in the teacher force and help sustain training institutions.

Education graduates — the new entrants to teaching — are traditionally the mainstay of teacher supply and are probably the one element of that supply most vulnerable to government policies and to changing job markets. The output of graduates will be higher, other things equal, the shorter the programs of study. Two-year accreditation, for example, will supply more teachers than three years of preparation. And as the teacher stock itself is subject to attrition, so the number of new entrants to teaching may be fewer than those initially enrolled. At least four kinds of "wastage" may occur: drop-out from the program, year repetition, examination failure, and failure to enter teaching.

* * *

Although overall teacher demand and supply may match, there still may be pockets of surplus or shortage in particular regions or in certain courses. Geographical immobility will keep teachers and jobs apart. And insufficient knowledge of certain school subjects by teachers will produce shortages within an overall setting of demand-supply equality. Unesco's International Institute for Educational Planning underscores this reality:

If teachers and teaching jobs were completely undifferentiated, it would be satisfactory to work at this aggregate level, for teachers would be infinitely substitutable for each other. In fact, however, teaching jobs are to some extent differentiated and many of them can be performed only by teachers with certain characteristics. The market for teachers is not one unified market, but a collection of partially self-contained smaller markets.[4]

A shift in any of the components of demand or supply can cause a discrepancy between the number of teaching posts and the numbers of teachers ready to fill them. Although an array of constituents determines supply and demand, and precipitates such conditions as teacher redundancy, the commonly touted

---

[4] Peter Williams, *Planning Teacher Demand and Supply* (1979), p. 80.

culprit in Canada is declining enrolment. But whatever the cause or causes of over-staffed schools, the effects are far-reaching.

The effects

Redundancy certainly has implications for teacher well-being, the recruitment and deployment of teaching personnel, and the preference for term and part-time appointments. But its effects reach beyond manpower economics to the morale of teachers and faculty of education students, to the chance for new avenues of instruction, to changes in the quality of education, and to modifications in curriculum and school objectives.

Morale In a time of high expectations and assumed well-being, failure to find work is unsettling, particularly for university graduates such as teachers who have years of effort invested in what they thought was an essential and stable future. Speaking to the 56th annual convention of the Canadian Education Association in Winnipeg, September 26, 1979, University of Alberta President Myer Horowitz said enrolments at the university's faculty of education are only 40 per cent of what they were six years earlier because prospective teachers are afraid of graduating only to be unemployed. Students at the Queen's University faculty of education in Kingston were quoted in the Kingston *Whig Standard*, January 9, 1979, as saying education students are naive. "We're all idiots here," said one student. "Anybody who gets involved in education at a time like this is an idiot. When we're practice teaching, teachers at our schools tell us we're crazy."

The students have grounds for their concerns. A yet-unpublished Statistics Canada survey of education graduates, who were accredited in 1976 and polled in 1978, found 3.9 per cent of them out of work, while 69.5 per cent of those employed had found jobs as elementary or secondary teachers. The majority of the rest had positions only partly connected to their studies. And 9 per cent found their university training unrelated to their employment.

The prospect of unemployment is often more disruptive than its eventuality. The teacher facing the spectre of his own redundancy must continue to inspire his class and nurture his professional growth while puzzling over his financial security and scanning the job market for alternatives. The pressure is bound to affect output and student performance, according to

Ontario's Commission on Declining Enrolments:

When they think about declining enrolment, teachers worry about losing their jobs. This kind of worry is stressful and likely to retard the efficiency of even those teachers who retain their jobs.[5]

Supervisors also must struggle with the consequences of demoralized teachers. According to an Ontario study[6], supervisory officers responding to a questionnaire on the effects of redundancy emphasized the substantial attention they currently pay to the realized and potential impact of teacher insecurity and job dissatisfaction among educators in that province.

School students' morale could slip too as fewer course options in the face of austerity dampen general student interest in the program. Any loss of special education courses may well have a negative effect on the retention rate and feelings of inadequacy by low-achievers.

Programs In a survey of almost 200 Ontario school boards and about 1,000 teachers, a CODE working paper[7] found several changes in objectives and programs expected in the wake of redundancy.

At the primary level, two-thirds of affected boards expect to be harmed by declining enrolments over the next four years. Creative arts and language arts are most likely to fall prey to cutbacks, with a quarter of all boards anticipating the dropping or consolidation of music, drama, physical education, writing, and visual arts programs. A quarter of all boards expect changes in the amount of classroom time spent by students on music, visual arts, values, decision-making, speaking, and reading. Nearly one-half of responding boards foresee changed availability of special programs such as remedial, enrichment, and extra-curricular activities, especially in arithmetic, reading, speaking, music, listening, writing, physical education, geometry, and drama. About a third of the boards predict a changed supply of specially trained staff in arithmetic, music, physical education, science and geography, drama, visual arts, speaking, and writing.

---

[5] David E. Hunt and Janice S. Hunt, *On the Psychology of Declining Enrolment: With a Brief Review of Attempts to Cushion the Negative Effects of Professional Unemployment* (1978), pp. 8-9.

[6] K. Leithwood and D. Montgomery, *Effects of Declining Enrolments on the Curriculum: Perceptions of Supervisory Officers* (1978).

[7] Robin J. Enns, et al., *The Effect of Declining Enrolment on School Objectives and Programs* (1979).

One-half of junior high boards forecast redundancy working to the detriment of creative arts and language arts programs, with consolidation or elimination of music, physical education, speaking, and values competency. A fifth of the boards expect changes in classroom time devoted to content in music, physical education, speaking, visual arts, listening, health and decision-making, and a third see changes in remedial, enrichment, and extra-curricular activities, namely music, physical education, and reading. As well, a third see changes in the stock of teachers trained in music, physical education, visual arts, and speaking.

Three-quarters of boards expect changes at the intermediate and senior levels in their offering of official languages, general and multidisciplinary studies, and business studies, with a quarter of them foretelling cuts or groupings in Spanish, physical and health education, group guidance, environmental science, German, and consumer studies.

Changes expected in school board organization are mainly the consolidating and twinning of boards, and reductions in superintendencies, consultant contracts, and number of schools. Boards expect more split grades and program integration, fewer department heads, vice-principals and resources staff, and less school administration time. Boards are also planning for an expansion of bilingual programs, greater teacher reliance on textbooks, and a decline in experimental courses and equipment availability in music, industrial arts, science, and the arts.

According to the boards surveyed, there will be more student evaluation and special training outside regular classrooms, and a reduction in field trips and extra-curricular activity.

Curriculum According to research[8] by the CODE, curriculum support staff numbers have fallen dramatically because of teacher redundancy. The loss of resource teachers, consultants, and co-ordinators, for example, will mean loss of the main source of instructional help for teachers. Fewer and smaller curriculum writing teams will mean fewer on-the-job professional development opportunities for the teachers who would have staffed those teams.

School principals, seen as curriculum leaders in elementary schools, are expected to fill the gap left by cutbacks in curriculum support staff, yet they already face a mounting workload as schools are combined and vice-principal positions abolished.

---

[8] K. Leithwood and D. Montgomery, op.cit.

According to the report, shrinking Ontario schools will provide fewer courses and levels at which courses could be offered. French immersion and special education programs are in jeopardy at the elementary level. Creative writing and geometry at the junior level may suffer as well. But advantages stemming from redundancy in Ontario might include concentration on more limited and realistic goals by schools, and more pressure for community consultation by boards.

Quality The excess of teacher supply over demand could foster more selective teacher recruitment through more stringent criteria for entry into the profession. According to the OECD[9], the future could see greater emphasis on a candidate's previous social experience, maturity, and motives for choosing a teaching career. Boards may also raise formal qualifications for teachers, a move which the OECD says will boost educational quality. And faculties of education may stiffen their admission requirements.

At the Memorial University of Newfoundland's faculty of education, admission procedures already have changed, favouring more discretion on the part of the faculty selection committee and less student self-selection.

Admission to the Faculty of Education at Memorial prior to Spring 1977 simply involved a student indicating on a form from the Registrar's Office that he or she wanted to be in the Faculty of Education in one of the degree programs offered. Acceptance was primarily an adminstrative function on the part of the Office of the Registrar, in which the staff checked whether or not the student met the academic criteria set down in the admission regulations.

* * *

The present procedure for admission to the Faculty of Education has changed, therefore, in that interested students complete a more comprehensive application that includes the student's personal statement as to why he wishes to train to be a teacher and what he believes he can contribute to the teaching profession, and requires the student to obtain two referees who will forward to the Co-ordinator of Student Selection and Advising letters of reference on the student's behalf. These letters of reference provide an overview of the applicant's personal characteristics and suitability for teaching.[10]

The OECD points out that U.S. opinion favours a first university degree plus two or three years' professional training and teaching practice. England and Wales are expecting the

[9] Organisation for Economic Co-operation and Development. *op. cit.*

[10] E.J. Cluett and F. Buffett, eds., *Report of the Conference on Declining Enrolments: Implications for Teacher Supply and Demand* (1979), pp. 30-31.

number of teacher trainees taking a fourth year of studies to increase, and are considering phasing-out non-graduate teacher training courses in favour of degree programs.

According to the CODE, redundancy could trigger loss of professional development opportunities, job insecurity, reduced specialization, and fewer instructional materials. This development would lead to less indvidualized student attention, less student grouping for instruction, and fewer field trips. In consequence, less enthusiastic teachers would be working with less ardent students. A scarcity of curriculum guidance for teachers and an emphasis on textbooks to the exclusion of other learning resources would aggravate this condition.

Fewer teachers have enriched the quality of education in some Ontario schools. Boards are relying more on community resources in the arts, notably in music and drama; cultural groups have been volunteering their services and saving boards money.

Costs Teacher costs per pupil are certain to rise due to redundancy, even in the absence of lower pupil-teacher ratios and substantial salary hikes, according to Unesco[11]. The culprit is "qualification inflation", a by-product of the higher standards faculties and boards will be tempted to introduce. As better candidates enter teacher training, the composition of the teacher force will shift from the lower to the higher salary scales. This trend will accelerate if boards are replacing under-qualified teachers with better-educated candidates, a process likely to occur as deficient teachers are released during redundancy, then replaced by superior graduates when budgets loosen or when teacher demand rises. The impact on costs will be particularly pronounced where teacher salaries depend more on qualifications than responsiblity. Exaggerating this tendency will be the aging of the teacher force after the period of rapid expansion. As teachers grow older, "incremental creep", as Unesco calls it, will see the "average teacher" salary point move from the lower to the upper end of the scale; during this period, entry of new teachers at lower salaries will be insufficient to steady the average age and, therefore, hold salary growth to only the rate of inflation.

So, there is a built-in cost escalation in teachers' salaries, independent of enrolments or contract settlements. In an attempt to counter this bias, boards may constrain budgets through measures they know might harm the quality of

---

[11] Peter Williams, op.cit.

education. They may raise the number of students per teacher, thus damping teacher recruitment. Or, they may decide to favour less well-qualified and, therefore, cheaper candidates.

Supply teachers When money is tight and demand scarce, firms often rely on short-term measures to sustain their viability. These may include policies of leasing, not buying, facilities, and term contracts for staff. Such manoeuvers promote essential flexibility and may, in fact, encourage better performance from employees not assured of a permanent position. The strategy has application in the teaching sector in the the form of supply or substitute teachers:

Quite apart from the possibility that they may be cheaper to employ, temporary teachers are also often more willing to serve in difficult posts. To keep a pool of temporary appointments in a teaching force (even if the individual incumbents of those temporary posts change) can provide a much needed flexibility in responding to changes in demand arising from unpredictable trends such as population shifts. There is much to be said for planning a teacher force with only 85-95 per cent permanent and pensionable employees, rather than aiming for the full 100 per cent.[12]

The teacher force As more teachers forego early retirement and as enrolments in faculties of education decline, turnover in the teacher force is lower and its composition doesn't change nearly as much. Consequently, the teacher force in Canada is aging.

The rapid growth of education in the 1960s has left the teaching profession with a block of young teachers who will comprise the dominant age group for some time. As they age, there will undoubtedly arise a climate of stability in teacher supply and better course continuity from one year to the next as more people make teaching a lifetime career. According to one school of thought, the most creative teachers are 30 to 45 years of age. With half of Manitoba's teachers, for example, in this age group, methods of instruction should become more progressive.

Others argue aging is accompanied by conservatism and a lack of imagination. To the extent aging and low turnover retard experimentation and innovation, and to the extent teacher populations in other provinces correspond to that of Manitoba, boards and governments may devote more resources to certification renewal, to funding innovative programs, and to teacher exchanges and sabbaticals. Education institutions will also have a responsibility to

---

[12] Unesco, *op. cit.*, p. 50.

prepare young teachers to cope with resistance to change.

Such uneven growth and aging of teacher supply will cause other difficulties in the long term. There will be an imbalance not only in age but in quality. If large numbers of teachers are hired when educational requirements and training course quality are low, followed by smaller groups of teachers with superior qualifications, the slowing of expansion will cause problems. There will be far fewer opportunities for promotion, and if advancement is based on seniority, morale among young teachers may dwindle. Boards will face more serious management problems during slow growth or contraction than during expansion, particularly as they try to achieve a good distribution of staff between individual schools, school districts, and subject specialties. The distorted age structure will also cause administrative difficulty at retirement. The pattern of retirements will reflect the uneven rate of recruitment — erratic hiring will eventually cause large exoduses of staff as blocks of teachers reach retirement age.

* * *

As the supply of teachers has outpaced the demand for them several other effects have made themselves felt. School boards are promoting part-time teaching and early retirement, extended leave without pay, professional development, and reassignment. Teacher federations, in conjunction with boards, are sponsoring career workshops for teachers leaving the profession. And there has been a growing awareness of, if not an emphasis on, adult and pre-school education and special education as areas chronically in need of attention and which could help balance teacher supply and demand. Following a discussion of the mechanisms for equating supply and demand, Chapters 4 and 5 examine the various attempts at aiding the redundant teacher.

Chapter 3
Combatting teacher redundancy

Although existing overall redundancy is not preventable, poor distribution of teachers can be relieved and potential shortages avoided through strategies of supply and demand management and through long-term data collection and planning.

Supply

In any industrialized economy, there are rapid and continuing changes in tastes, incomes, and technology, and there are shifts in preference for one good or service to another. These movements trigger a relentless flow of workers among occupations. Countless new jobs are posted; people are hired and fired; people quit and retire; firms fail and jobs vanish. This process of adjustment costs time and money and a great deal of energy and persistence.

More money, time, and effort than necessary will be expended if the market's match-making is impeded in any way. Many workers have only an incomplete view of job openings and many employers have only limited information on the numbers and qualifications of prospective employees. These flaws — economists call them market imperfections — may bring about so-called "structural unemployment" and "bottlenecks" which hinder the progress of the economy. Structural unemployment takes hold when the need for a product, and therefore a worker, dries up. Bottlenecks prevail when the excessive manpower can't shift smoothly to another field; workers become redundant, alternative employment elusive.

But it is not only the labour market that can fail at its task. The mechanisms available to the job-seeker may be faulty. A worker trying to match his skills and potential to a new occupation must finance that search; he may even require retraining and a move to a new location. These steps are costly, yet the unemployed worker may have trouble borrowing on the security of his own track record, and an uncertain future may discourage his going into debt.

Several strategies can streamline the manpower allocation process, benefiting both job-seeker and employer. These include:

• a sound educational preparation, with emphasis on breadth and versatility;
• selective recruitment with an eye to practical skills and performance;
• on-the-job improvement;
• retraining programs to cope with technological change or change in demand;
• maximum geographical mobility, enhanced dissemination of job opening details and information on the available labour force; and
• research and planning of labour needs and how best to meet them.

Using these methods as guidelines, those responsible for recruiting and managing a teacher force can avoid pitfalls common to their area and remedy several problems they currently face.

The broader a teacher's education, the less likely he is to become trapped in a field for which there is no demand. The outlets for a specialist are few and his costs of retraining substantial. Aware of this danger, the faculty of education at Queen's University in Kingston has introduced new subjects into its curriculum to attract new kinds of students and discover new employment markets for its graduates. The versatility of the faculty's education students will be strengthened by their preparation for work beyond the classroom in settings such as senior citizens' homes, jails, personnel offices, and homes for the retarded.

In the wake of the new policy, Queen's has found teaching jobs for 65 per cent of its 1979 graduates. Another 15 per cent have accepted employment in non-teaching jobs or returned to university. Yet only 33 per cent of the 1979 graduates from all Ontario teacher training institutions have found jobs in publicly supported Ontario schools.

Other universities as well are changing programs to enhance the employability of their graduates. The faculty of education at the University of Alberta in Edmonton, for example, relies on a broad-based program with emphasis on a common core of instruction for students of both elementary and secondary education, but with a new twist. An approach begun four years ago at the university and only now making itself felt stresses the concept of a "second major" or a "minor" subject to "broaden the capability of graduates", according to Dr. Robert Patterson, associate dean of the faculty. The choice among options rests entirely with the student; the university advises freshmen on shortages in such subjects as hard sciences and music, and on an over-abundance in history and English, hoping they will choose a program of study accordingly.

At the University of Saskatchewan in Regina, the notion of three specialties is gaining credence. The university's new elementary program stresses specialization in reading and two other areas of the student's choice. Students may also concentrate on subjects in both the elementary and secondary levels.

Perceptive and cautious recruitment is essential, too. Teacher selection and assignment are critical steps in assuring an efficient education enterprise. The selection process should eliminate teacher candidates who will be ineffective in practice, and assignments should match teacher to task for best performance.

On-the-job improvement of professional standards through self-help or more formal programs is a key ingredient in maintaining an adaptable teacher force. A good deal of professional knowledge and competence is lost in the absence of continual efforts to upgrade. According to some, at least a quarter of one's knowledge dissipates in five years without steps to revitalize that knowledge.

If a teacher is to move within the educational system, either by choice or necessity, to a new course area or to a new responsibility such as administration, retraining will prove a most valuable catalyst. More than 15 years ago, economist Jacob Mincer noted the importance of practical knowledge gained beyond the formal education setting:

In the context of the economist's concern with education as a process of investment in manpower, it is important to be reminded that formal school instruction is neither an exclusive nor a sufficient method of training the labour force. Graduation from some level of schooling does not signify the completion of a training process. It is usually the end of a more general and preparatory stage, and the beginning of a more specialized and often prolonged process of acquisition of occupational skill, after entry into the labour force. This second stage, training on-the-job, ranges from formally organized activities such as apprenticeships and other training programs to the informal processes of learning from experience. Indeed, historically, skills have been acquired mainly by experience on the job. The vast schooling system and the delayed entry into the labour force are distinctly modern phenomena.[13]

A substitute for, and often a complement to, retraining is geographic mobility. As training promotes movement across occupational boundaries, so mobility involves spatial movement, each directed toward the same end — matching labour supply to demand. If, for example, redundancy threatens a teacher's job, he may either retrain for a different locally required skill in teaching or in a new field, or he may move to a different area where his present skills are still in demand. A social studies teacher bolstering his French knowledge in preparation for a new teaching assignment in that high demand area is following the first course. A physical education teacher who moves from Toronto, Ontario, to Berens River, Manitoba, to take up a teaching post in that same subject, is following the latter course.

Making a move at the right time and to the right place depends on thorough information about job openings being dispatched quickly throughout the potential recruitment area. Such agencies as federal employment centres and private counselling and job location firms are beneficial, but a special organization, designed expressly for teachers, could offer a further advantage in times of excess.

The Ontario Public School Men Teachers' Federation, in a brief to the CODE in 1978, called for a concerted effort at communicating job openings:

The availability of teaching positions to serve specific needs should be widely communicated across the province.... While many boards of education probably conduct assessment of staffing needs, these are probably not paired with talent or interest assessments of current staff. Nor are these assessments adequately communicated. A better

---

[13] Unesco, Readings in the Economics of Education (1968), p. 524.

alternative might be a system of provincial assessment coupled with a province-wide placement service that would attempt to match redundancies in one board with needs in another.[14]

A survey of unemployed teachers by the Institute for Educational Research and Development of the Memorial University of Newfoundland found 90 per cent of respondents in favour of a provincial registry of unemployed teachers to be used by boards in recruitment.

Education and relocation can be part of single redeployment strategy as well. In the case of teachers with obsolete skills, say a history specialty, living in an economically slack locality such as Gaspé, training and mobility would complement one another. And, of course, training may well enhance a worker's mobility.

These measures are aimed at the supply side of the market — they are means of fine-tuning the worker to the task. Economists speak of demand management policies as well.

Demand

In Sweden, for example, manpower policy controls many expenditures affecting the level and location of employment and thus influences the demand side of the market equation. Winter works as a scheme to even out seasonal fluctuations in demand, or to adjust regional patterns of government expenditure so as to re-allocate labour demand regionally, are examples of policies meant to smooth demand.

Applied to educators, such policies might take the form of expanding pre-school, adult, and special education to create a new market for excess teachers. They could also take the form of breaking down barriers to education by improving transportation to schools and helping parents with the indirect costs of educating their children, and permitting pupil re-entry, repetition of grades, and part-time attendance. As well, the average size of class could be reduced, and teacher hours per class could be increased, by offering more options, practical work, individual supervision, and remedial work. Overtime could be discouraged and non-teaching jobs in education could be expanded with a preference given to teachers. According to the Canadian Teachers' Federation, there is a wide variety of school-related occupations not involving regular classroom teaching. Specialized positions,

---

[14] Ontario Public School Men Teachers' Federation, *Brief to the Commission on Declining Enrolments* (1978), p. 22.

suited to individuals trained in education, include researchers in school boards and departments of education, consultants, curriculum development specialists, and staff members of teachers' organizations and other education associations. In other cases, school-related posts that do not rely on an education background include nursing, psychology, and social work. And, for people untrained and willing to learn on-the-job, there is the teacher aide position, involving clerical and minor instructional roles under the direction of teachers or principals. Some community colleges offer teacher aide preparation.

Planning

Planning and research — the investment of effort, not in the day-to-day demands of market adjustment, but in circumspect review of what that market is doing and how its performance can be improved — is essential to a healthy market for teachers. As early as 1964, the Economic Council of Canada pressed for manpower policies to "assist and promote adjustment to change". A year later, the federal agency emphasized "the need for urgent and prompt improvement in the field of labour market policy". In response, the Department of Manpower and Immigration came into being, comprising a section concerned solely with research, development, evaluation, and labour market information. Recognizing a criterion established by the Organisation for Economic Co-operation and Development that research account for at least one per cent of total manpower spending, the new department devoted more than that proportion to systematic analysis as a base for policy formation. School boards might do well to consider a similar emphasis on looking to the events of the future long before their arrival.

But there are obstacles board planners must surmount. Projections depend as much on assumptions as on calculations; and many assumptions depend on unknowns. So administrators would be well advised to plan for more than one eventuality, setting out a range of possible demand-supply values, one for each set of assumptions. Then, vigilant monitoring and adjustment of the estimates should occur, and, finally, planners should build options into the teacher supply system whch they can exercise as circumstances change and assumptions become obsolete. These safeguards include the capacity of teacher training institutions to serve a second purpose; teachers who can switch subjects or teach more than one; a reserve list of teachers willing to return to teaching full- or part-time if called on; and contacts with international teacher supply agencies.

Because a teacher's training and the course he is teaching may not correspond, sound estimates depend on tabulations of exactly how teachers are being used and the matching of assignments to specialties. The French teacher who is teaching mathematics should be treated as an unqualified teacher of mathematics, representing a loss from the trained group of French teachers.

The first step in wise planning, then, is to decide on a means of collecting, recording, and analyzing data on the stock of teachers and in changes in that stock. Then, boards should set up the mechanism for carrying out these functions. The specialist task of analyzing and forecasting teacher requirements should be assigned to an officer of the school board. Consultative ability of those chosen is critical, because so much of planning in any setting calls for communication and persuasion as much as it does technical expertise. This added quality will show its worth as the need grows to involve teachers, faculty, and the public in teacher planning.

* * *

Adherence to these general principles of labour supply and demand management will foster three goals, say the economists: growth, equity, and stabilization. Applied to the economy as a whole, these mean the long-run economic health of the country will improve (growth); poverty will be reduced and inter-regional disparities in people's incomes will shrink (equity); and unemployment will be reduced and price increases moderated (stabilization).

Applied to teaching, these goals may be expressed as maintenance of quality education in the long-term, avoidance of discrepancies among provinces in the worth of education and the qualifications and opportunities of teachers, and the curbing of teacher unemployment and jumps in the cost of education.

The goals, particularly those regarding preparation for a job and continued upgrading, can be promoted by the individual. But, as well, they are worth pursuing socially. Here, there is a role for government in bettering the labour force and planning its destiny, since (a) training often benefits more people than the individual taking it, (b) individuals often are without the resources to effect the improvement unaided, and because (c) there may well be economies associated with retraining large groups at a time, instead of pockets of teachers scattered among boards, which make it more efficient for government to initiate much of this activity.

Policies aimed at supply of teachers, not the demand, have been the focus of school boards seeking solutions to redundancy.

Chapter 4
Rerouting the redundant teacher within education

Many remedies for teacher redundancy have been tried or proposed in Canada, each with a varying measure of success. These range from simple upgrading of practical skills to actual dismissal. Along the spectrum of choice lie such partial solutions as part-time teaching, extended leave, retraining for a new career, overseas service, and expansion of the market through adult and pre-school education. Of course, no one option can be expected to be a complete solution.

Some of the policies for coping with a glut on the market for educational manpower are recent and, therefore, have undergone little assessment. Other measures, in place for some time, stand as examples for others to follow. This chapter reviews strategies to deal with redundant teachers while retaining them in the education system, and reports where possible on the success with which these programs have met. Chapter 5 considers the opportunities for teachers wishing to abandon their beleaguered profession in favour of either a new career or retirement.

Part-time teaching

After four years as a full-time teacher of French and art, Winnipeg teacher Mia Stepnuk switched to half-time instruction to devote more attention to her new-born child. Mia speaks highly of the advantages of part-time teaching.

"Teaching full-time in a large school, you don't have a minute to yourself; even in the staff room, you're not alone. Teaching part-time, you're not nearly as tired. Because you're not at that frazzled edge, you can deal with the kids better; and they stand to gain from that."

Mia finds time to prepare that she didn't have as a full-time teacher, and she has time to improve her own academic qualifications which she may apply either in teaching, or in another field.

Teachers speak of many more benefits of part-time teaching. Educators who might otherwise be unemployed or posted in the wilderness are often thankful for a part-time position which doesn't involve uprooting their families and affords them experience and an avenue into full-time teaching. And the salary is not proportionately less for the part-time teacher because the lower earnings mean a lower tax bracket and a greater percentage of take-home pay than the full-time professional receives.

The free time enjoyed by part-timers makes community involvement easier, encourages leisure-time activities, and permits the teacher to try alternative employment if he wishes. As well, teaching only a portion of each day is one way to ease into retirement.

Mia points out that she spends as much time with her students as she would if at school full-time. "Because their schedule coincides with mine, they don't see me less but I see fewer students." But the fact that Mia had already taught at the same school full-time makes the new role easier than it may be for someone new to his teaching institution.

"Had I gone to a new school, the workload would have been much greater, at least at first. Here, I know the kids, I know the other teachers, and I know the principal's expectations." In fact, Mia helped organize the program she now teaches. These are advantages the newcomer wouldn't share.

The benefits of part-time teaching accrue not only to the individual, but also to the system. Two half-time teachers will do more than simply comprise a single, full-time position, because the greater amount of time available to them for preparation brings much more creativity to bear on the job than a single full-timer could muster. The added time teachers are able to devote to non-teaching activities is likely to generate a greater breadth of experience upon which to draw when compiling lessons. And, according to the Burnaby Teachers' Association, pupils benefit from exposure to two personalities in the classroom, and from younger, more innovative teachers who are often able to get into a crowded teaching profession only because of a part-time arrangement.

But part-time teaching, whether for part of a year, part of a week, or part of each day, does have drawbacks for both the teacher and the administration.

"It's very difficult to leave the school when you're supposed to leave," says Winnipeg elementary teacher Timothy Rafter, who teaches eight-tenths of each day. "You find yourself staying around, working for free."

As a physical education teacher, Timothy finds coaching teams often to be an impingement on his own time. Most practices are after school hours, so on days when he finishes at 2:30 p.m., Timothy either must stay at the school or come back after going home. "Otherwise, it would be hard to explain to parents — 'I'm not getting paid for it so I'm not here'. The kids still don't know what I'm doing. They expect you to be there all the time."

And, because their contracts expire in June, part-time teachers must begin looking for fall-term work as early as February. The prospects are not always certain.

Adminstrators in Burnaby, Surrey, Coquitlam, and Vancouver, questioned in a survey about part-time arrangements, were uneasy about having more staff to contact and evaluate, and were concerned about consistent discipline and the willingness of part time teachers to engage in extra-curricular activities. But the energy of teachers like Timothy Rafter has eased this apprehension.

The part-time program of the Lakehead Board of Education in Thunder Bay sets out requirements which could be of some concern to teachers. The part-time teacher receives no guarantee of times he will be teaching from one year to the next, and the well-being of the students and the school in general take precedence over the choice of subjects or scheduling of the part-time teacher.

Co-operation of all staff is expected in co-curricular activities, and the onus is on the part-time teacher to be available for consultation with another teacher sharing his classroom to ensure a co-ordinated program. As well, part-time teachers must be willing to provide extra help for students neeeding tutorial assistance. According to the board, "Flexibility in scheduling is essential. Assistance may be provided to students before and after school or during the lunch break". Reporting to parents still commands as much of the part-time teacher's attention as that of the full-time teacher. The board stresses the importance of staff meetings, and encourages all teachers, full- or part-time, to attend. Occasions such as parents' nights, open houses, and graduations are to be attended by both part-time and full-time teachers.

Salary increases for part-time teachers at the Lakehead Board are different in the elementary and secondary grades. Because the elementary salary grid placement rounds fractions of years of experience up if that fraction is 0.5 or greater, and down if it is less than 0.5, salary adjustments occur at best only every two years, and as infrequently as every four years. See Tables 2 and 3, below.

Table 2

Grid placement of elementary teacher with three years' experience who switches to half-time in fourth year and continues to teach half-time

School years	Accumulation of experience	Salary grid placement	Annual salary scale
Year 4	3.0	Year 3	$15,750
Year 5	3.5	Year 4	16,550
Year 6	4.0	Year 4	16,550
Year 7	4.5	Year 5	17,350

Source: Lakehead Board of Education Task Force on Declining Enrolment, Sub-committee on Part-Time Teaching, *Part-Time Teaching: A Consideration in an Era of Declining Enrolment* (1979).

In Table 2, the teacher going into his fifth year of teaching is accorded 3.5 years of experience, his position on the salary grid is rated at four years, and the corresponding annual salary used to calculate his actual earnings jumps from $15,750 to $16,550 — the four-year figure. But moving into his sixth year, while his experience rating increases, his salary grid rating, and thus his salary, remain the same. It is not until his seventh year that his accumulated experience of 4.5 years is rounded up to a five-year grid placement, and a raise in pay results.

In Table 3, the teacher going into his fifth year encounters no change in salary since his accumulation of 3.25 years of experience is rounded back down to 3.0. In his sixth year, rounding up gives him a raise, but he remains at the new rating of $16,550 until his tenth year when rounding up again takes place.

At the secondary level, although a teaching time of half a year or more moves the teacher to the next highest point on the grid — the same procedure as for elementary remuneration — if the fraction is less than 0.5, the teacher is paid that fraction of the salary increment, unlike the practice for teachers of primary grades; salary adjustment is thus continuous. So, there is a built-in incentive, at least at schools operated by the Lakehead Board, to teach secondary grades or to teach at least half-time or more in the elementary grades if regular salary adjustment is important to the teacher.

Table 3

Grid placement of elementary teacher with three years' experience who switches to one-quarter time in fourth year and continues to teach one-quarter time

School years	Accumulation of experience	Salary grid placement	Annual salary scale
Year 4	3.0	Year 3	$15,750
Year 5	3.25	Year 3	15,750
Year 6	3.5	Year 4	16,550
Year 7	3.75	Year 4	16,550
Year 8	4.0	Year 4	16,550
Year 9	4.25	Year 4	16,550
Year 10	4.5	Year 5	17,350

Source: Lakehead Board of Education Task Force on Declining Enrolment, Sub-committee on Part-Time Teaching, *Part-Time Teaching: A Consideration in an Era of Declining Enrolment* (1979).

One of the most serious drawbacks of part-time teaching, especially as a route to early retirement, is the effect the reduced service has on future pension earnings. Because annual pension is equal to 70 per cent of a teacher's average salary over his best seven years at Lakehead, switching to part-time toward the end of one's career can reduce superannuation earnings, as Table 4 illustrates.

In this example, Teacher A teaches full-time until retirement, reaching a best-seven-year average salary of $22,795, while Teacher B switches from full- to half-time for the last two years of his career, reaching a $21,049 average. Consequently, Teacher A's annual pension, based on 35 years' service, is $15,956.50, while Teacher B's yearly pension earnings amount to $14,734.30, about $100 a month less than his full-time colleague.

This disadvantage to part-time can be greater or less, depending on the period over which provincial regulations calculate the annual salary average for retirement purposes. In Alberta, for example, a best-five-year average is used. So the teacher working part-time for two years at the end of his career would lower his average, and therefore his pension, even further in that province than in Ontario.

Table 4

Comparison of the average salaries over the best seven years of full- and part-time teachers

School year	Salary maximum	Teacher A	Average salary	Teacher B	Average salary
1969-70	$14,700	—	—	—	—
70-71	15,400	—	—	—	—
71-72	15,900	—	—	—	—
72-73	16,500	—	—	—	—
73-74	17,325	Full-	—	Full-	—
74-75	20,400	time	—	time	—
75-76	23,610		—		—
76-77	25,494		—		
77-78	27,300		$20,932	Part-	$20,082
78-79	28,938		22,795	time	21,049

Source: Lakehead Board of Education Task Force on Declining Enrolment, Sub-committee on Part-Time Teaching, *Part-Time Teaching: A Consideration in an Era of Declining Enrolment* (1979).

An equally awkward stumbling block to part-time employment is its effect on one's retirement gratuity, according to Lakehead officials. In that jurisdiction, a lump-sum payment, based on accumulated sick days not taken and on salary, accrues to the teacher at retirement. Half-time service prior to retirement cuts that gratuity in half, costing the teacher as much as $7,500 in foregone earnings.

Despite the drawbacks, part-time teaching is gaining a following. Prince Edward Island's Unit One school board has found teachers agreeable to working half-years. If the program goes ahead, some teachers will work from September to February, while others will be in the classroom from February to June.

A spring 1979 survey of 240 teachers in seven of Ontario's Niagara South high schools showed 28 per cent willing to consider sharing their jobs with other teachers under various conditions.

At the London Board, a part-time teaching program attracted 15 teachers in 1979, and saved eight jobs. And a variation of part-time employment — job sharing — has been successful in Oromocto, New Brunswick. Planned during 1978-79, and launched in the 1979-80 term, the pilot project requires two School District No. 25 teachers to work two and one-half days a week each, sharing all responsibilities, including courses, registers, reporting, and extra-curricular activities, of their grade six class of about 30 students. Sharing is carried to the letter, with each teacher presenting one-half of each course. According to Pat Thurber of the local school district, students and parents are pleased with the experiment. And so are the teachers. One has a young and growing family she wishes to spend more time with. And the other is reducing her workload with an eye to retirement.

Table 5

Part-time teaching by province*, 1972-73 and 1978-79

	1972-73		1978-79	
	Number of teachers	Per cent of all teachers	Number of teachers	Per cent of all teachers
Newfoundland	16	0.2%	50	0.6%
Prince Edward Island	27	1.8	47	3.2
Nova Scotia	85	0.8	119	1.1
New Brunswick	117	1.5	207	2.6
Ontario	2321	2.4	6458	6.4
Manitoba	394	3.3	678	5.5
Saskatchewan	360	3.2	777	6.7
Alberta	624	3.0	1193	5.1
British Columbia	641	2.9	1877	6.6
Northwest Territories	6	1.0	7	1.0
Yukon	1	0.4	28	9.5
Total:	**4592**	**2.4**	**11,431**	**5.6**

*Data for Quebec unavailable.
Source: C.T. Curteis, Education, Science, and Culture Division, Statistics Canada, Ottawa. Unpublished paper (November 1979).

Part-time teachers comprised only 2.4 per cent of the teacher force in 1972-73, but by 1978-79 the percentage was 5.6, according to Statistics Canada. The growing appeal of part-time instruction has been nation-wide, but the western provinces and Ontario have displayed a stronger move in that direction than has Atlantic Canada. See Table 5 (p. 41).

The movement of teachers from full- to part-time, and from part- to full-time, has been substantial. As Table 6, below, shows, 2,329 teachers, four-fifths of them women, who taught full-time in 1977-78, taught part-time in 1978-79. Moving from part-time to full-time over the same period were 2,170 teachers,

Table 6

Elementary and secondary teachers shifting from part- to full-time or from full- to part-time, each as a proportion of all teachers changing status over the period 1977-78 to 1978-79***

	Full-time 1977-78 to Part-time 1978-79	Part-time 1977-78 to Full-time 1978-79
Elementary		
Male	210	186
%	12	12
Female	1510	1415
%	88	88
Total	1720	1601
%	74	74
Secondary		
Male	228	248
%	37	44
Female	381	321
%	63	56
Total	609	569
%	26	26
Total		
Male	438	434
%	19	20
Female	1891	1736
%	81	80
Total	2329	2170

*Data for Quebec unavailable

Source: C.T. Curteis, Education, Science, and Culture Division, Statistics Canada, Ottawa. Unpublished paper (November 1979).

(again four-fifths of them were women). Women dominated the shift either way at the elementary level, comprising nearly nine-tenths of all teachers changing their status over the period in question. At the secondary level, however, just over one-half of those altering their working time were women. Overall, of the teacher force who moved between full- and part-time, three-quarters taught elementary grades, and the remainder were secondary teachers.

According to Statistics Canada, 81 per cent of all part-time employment occurs at the elementary level, and 94 per cent of all part-time teachers are women. And, more than 90 per cent of all teachers changing their hours of work remained with the same school board.

Further, a sixth of all new teachers in 1978-79 were employed part-time, three times the proportion of all teachers engaged in part-time employment. Table 7 presents a provincial breakdown of the employment status of new recruits.

Table 7

Employment status of new teachers by province 1978-79*

	Full-time	Part-time	Total	Part-time as % of total
Newfoundland	724	24	748	3.2%
Prince Edward Island	108	14	122	11.5
Nova Scotia	908	40	948	4.2
New Brunswick	536	73	609	12.0
Ontario	5172	1295	6467	20.0
Manitoba	1054	158	1212	13.0
Saskatchewan	1234	239	1473	16.2
Alberta	2520	401	2921	13.7
British Columbia	2240	535	2775	19.3
Northwest Territories	61	9	70	12.9
Yukon	127	4	131	3.1
Total:	**14,684**	**2792**	**17,476**	**16.0**

*Data for Quebec unavailable
Source: C.T. Curteis, Education, Science, and Culture Division, Statistics Canada, Ottawa. Unpublished paper (November 1979).

Part-time employment in the teaching profession is occurring more and more frequently in the staffing of many Canadian schools. A clear preference for the lesser load has emerged over the past six years as thousands of practising educators reduce their hours of work, and as a growing proportion of newcomers to teaching share their responsibilities with colleagues.

The numbers of teachers moving from part-time to full-time suggest educators may be using a quarter-, half-, or three-quarter-time position as an avenue into full-time teaching. Correspondingly, those moving the other way are showing the potential partial employment holds for easing into retirement or devoting more time to homemaking, leisure, or study.

While the willingness of employed teachers to consider job sharing and of new recruits to accept part-time employment can certainly contribute to absorbing redundant or unemployed teachers, the strategy is largely short-term. Once the potential of the teacher force to relinquish earnings and the capacity of the system to take on additional manpower is reached, a certainty in the short-term, the ability to accommodate more teachers will shrink. While the pool of unemployed teachers can rise continually, their absorption by the school system reaches its limit in the short-term when everyone who wants to work part-time is working part-time. In the longer term, some part-time openings will occur, but at a much slower rate. Until then, however, part-time employment stands as one remedy to the problem of a bloated teacher supply.

The need for alternatives

The entire redundancy scare may be more apparent than real if some statistics are to be believed. Thousands of Canadian adults are illiterate, yet insufficient resources have been allocated to that problem or to adult education generally. Education of the retarded, handicapped, and gifted child is deficient. And expansion of pre-school instruction is not occurring on a wide scale.

Yet, in some provinces, pools of teacher manpower lie untapped, certified but out of work. Many more are standing at the front of classrooms they don't expect to see in the next school year. The existence of a stock of manpower, already largely trained to the task and available to be diverted to alternative education, presents a new opportunity to meet the educational needs of these special groups.

Adult education Opportunities for working people to improve their vocational qualifications are far from ideal in Canada. Adult illiteracy is also a serious problem. And, there is a need among union representatives for education which will prepare them for the rigours of collective bargaining. These were among the principal findings of the Report of the Commission of Inquiry on Educational Leave and Productivity, published in June, 1979[15].

The Commission concluded that an expansion of educational leave would be an appropriate and, in some cases, a necessary means of shoring up deficiencies in adult education. Taking such action would, of course, create a need for educators, a need redundant teachers, if equipped with some professional reorientation, could help meet.

Vocational education Vocational qualifications are an important determinant of a worker's earning power, job security, and social status, yet vocational training opportunities are insufficient at the secondary level. This limitation leaves only full-time post-secondary institutions as the location for serious vocational development, since most training in industry is short-term, job-specific, and available only to a minority, say the Adams Report commissioners.

From the point of view of the redundant teacher, and of the overstaffed school board, deficiencies in vocational education are good news, and the potential market for instructors is substantial. According to the Adams Commission, most Canadian adults have not had the benefit of any post-secondary education, nor do they enjoy employer-sponsored training because of the dependence of industry on post-secondary education graduates. The report points to skilled trade shortages in aerospace, automotive, cement and concrete, textiles and clothing, electrical, and machinery production areas, and to shortages of managerial and supervisory talent in textiles and clothing, commercial printing, construction, food and beverage, footwear, furniture manufacture, and restaurant and food services.

Such shortfalls in the labour market and their implications for the redeployment of educational manpower could offer an alternative to teachers wishing to explore new challenges within their profession.

Illiteracy One million Canadians can't read or write. Another four million haven't developed these skills far enough to function adequately in society. These estimates by Cairns[16] mean illiteracy is a greater problem than commonly thought.

---

[15] Commission of Inquiry on Educational Leave and Productivity, R.J. Adams, Chairman, *Education and Working Canadians; Report* (1979).

[16] J.C. Cairns, "Adult Functional Illiteracy in Canada," *Convergence,* vol. 10, no. 1, 1977, pp. 43-52.

And the problem goes beyond the obvious drawback of not being able to read a newspaper or a food package label.

Many illiterates are unemployed and on welfare, burdening the public purse. Aware of their shortcomings, many don't even bother to look for work. And a great many are below the poverty line. Because of their communication handicap, illiterates can be more accident prone and more of a drain on health care insurance and workers' compensation funds.

The federal Department of Employment and Immigration offers an array of programs designed for the under-educated, including Basic Training for Skill Development to strengthen mathematical, scientific, and communication skills, Basic Job Readiness Training, an employment-oriented course, and Work Adjustment Training, which helps reduce obstacles to finding and keeping employment. But, according to the Adams report, the courses aren't enough.

They are available almost exclusively to unemployed adults. Trainees may not attend school for more than a year, whether they need the added education or not. And there is no co-ordination of this training with that offered by diploma-granting institutions. Compounding these deficiencies, the Department of Employment and Immigration now prefers applicants to be better educated initially so they will benefit sooner from the government's courses; emphasis has shifted away from the seriously under-educated.

With this widening gap between the need for vocational upgrading and the supply of cheap, accessible, and long-term training, the demand for adult educators will persist, and a new opportunity for redundant teachers will prevail. Indeed, teaching Canada's illiterate could absorb every redundant teacher in the country.

Trade union training Union members depend on their elected representatives to negotiate and police contracts, and to document and present grievances, yet few union representatives have the appropriate education. Knowledge not only of the collective agreement, but of a variety of legislation and of the political and economic impact of union action, is essential, yet, according to the Adams report, it is lacking among union representatives, and the means of bridging this gap in knowledge are limited.

Historically, union training has taken place at night or on weekends, and has been confined to the large industrial unions with most sessions lasting an average of 12 hours. Professional and managerial employees have been four times as likely as non-office employees to receive extended leave for union studies, and three times as likely to be able to take time off from work for shorter periods.

Despite a five-year, $10 million agreement between Labour Canada and the Canadian Labour Congress in 1977 for the support of union education, and a further $300,000 education grant to unions not affiliated with the CLC, a large number of union representatives receive no training, according to the Adams report. Only a small minority enjoy advanced training. And fewer still have been educated to desirable standards. The Commission suggests there remains a good deal still to be done, and, with as many as 170,000 union representatives and local union officers in Canada, there should be considerable scope for redundant teachers to direct their energies toward bettering the quality of education in the labour movement, once the mechanisms to do so are in place.

Other adult education The findings of a CODE working paper[17] point to further evidence of educational needs among adults and suggest some ways school boards might meet that need. As well as illiterates, union representatives, and the vocationally deficient, there are adults who face retirement, female adults, immigrants, natives, and handicapped adults. Each has special educational requirements.

Older adults need accessible, convenient, varied, and free instruction. Wishing to keep healthy and financially secure, the older adult requires courses in health, nutrition, and planning for retirement. And, to maintain their self-esteem and feeling of belonging, the aging adults stand to benefit from education in personal growth and development, recreational and social activities, and in skills which will benefit their community. The working paper recommended that boards of education make an effort to meet these needs through engaging quality instructors, offering a counselling service suited to the older learner, and modifying their facilities to accommodate the particular disabilities of older adults.

Women, too, pose a special concern to the adult educator. Their passage through several distinct phases as families come and go and careers are abandoned and re-entered generates a need for instruction in child and family management, occupational preparation and academic upgrading, and decision-making skills. Research has shown women to favour greater flexibility in admission policies, residency require-ments, attendance requirements, and class scheduling. The

[17] Lynn Davie, et al., *Educational Needs and Learning Conditions of Adult Learners* (1978).

working paper recommended that institutions offer a broad range of credit and non-credit courses to women in literacy, academic upgrading, occupational training, and in areas of special interest to immigrant and ethnic women, and employ at least one person responsible solely for the concerns of women students.

The new immigrants, on the other hand, require problem-oriented education, addressing their needs for useful information, language skills, occupational preparation, and assessment of their foreign academic credentials and work experience. Once settled, the immigrant's concerns are more related to improving his language facility, job performance, and general ability to blend into his Canadian community while maintaining his ethnic identity. The working paper recommends that boards of education expand programs for immigrant learners, emphasizing English as a second language, academic upgrading, counselling services, and Canadian customs and life skills. It also suggests they strive to evaluate and certify educational credits and certificates and licences, professional credentials, and work experience that are not Canadian.

Quebec administers centres designed to assimilate the immigrant population for French instruction. The centres offer intensive French for new arrivals to the province, and "welcoming classes" for youngsters. The centres are an outlet for teachers out of work, and many tenured teachers have been drafted to staff these programs.

The pressing educational need of native people is that of basic literacy, according to the working paper, followed by alcohol-related programs, job skill improvement, including training for school committees and local government, and the preservation of native culture. According to research based on the 1971 census[18], there were 99,000 functionally illiterate native Canadians that year. With sizable proportions of natives in penal institutions, jail becomes an important setting for basic education, says the working paper.

Handicapped adults also seek to better their language skills, their ability to manage home and money, and their incomes according to two U.S. studies.[19]

---

[18] A.M. Thomas, *Adult Basic Education and Literacy Activities in Canada, 1975-76* (1976).

[19] S.A. Block, *Adult Education for the Deaf of Illinois: A Needs Assessment,* (Jacksonville, Illinois: Illinois Association of the Deaf, 1973), and E. Costello, "Continuing Education for Deaf Adults: A National Needs Assessment," *American Annals of the Deaf,* 1977, 122, (1), p. 26-32, cited in Davie, *op. cit.*

Special education The need for special education — the teaching of children with learning disabilities, behavioural problems, multiple handicaps — is rising in Canada.

In the mid-1960s, the Dominion Bureau of Statistics (DBS) found 10-15 per cent of Canadian children under age 19 suffering from some type of emotional or learning disorder. At the beginning of the 1970s, the Commission on Emotional and Learning Disorders in Children found 12-16 per cent of the youth population to be exceptional in some way, and claimed the figure could be as high as 25 per cent, depending on the definition used. Yet, according to the DBS study, only 2 per cent of children across Canada were enrolled in special education.

In Ontario, although total elementary enrolments are down, special education enrolments are up; thousands are on waiting lists and many more thousands are yet unidentified.

Several demographic, medical, and philosophical factors are responsible for there being more children requiring special education. There has been an increase in the number of premature infants who are surviving. Their low birth weight often leads to critical health problems which, in turn, obstruct their learning ability. Medical advances are enabling more children to survive illness or trauma, but survival often means severe multiple handicaps. Identification of the special child is becoming more thorough and there is a growing belief, first evidenced in the U.S., that services to handicapped children should occur earlier in their lives. These advancements are increasing the population for which special programming might be developed. With the emerging view that much of these children's education should occur in the regular classroom, not in special classes in special schools, the implications of special education for the redundant teacher, indeed all teachers, become clearer.

Pre-school education Pre-school education is the subject of growing interest as teachers look for new markets for their talents. Administrators and researchers have suggested making kindergarten compulsory and expanding the opportunities for offering pre-kindergarten classes.

As Table 8 shows, there is considerable room for an expansion of pre-schooling in Canada. As a rule-of-thumb, jurisdictions with a formal public pre-school system usually find most of their five-year-olds and virtually none of their four-year-olds enrolled in that system. Thus, an enrolment-population ratio of about 50 per cent indicates a developed system for five-year-olds.

According to this standard, Prince Edward Island, New Brunswick, and Alberta are relatively undeveloped in the field of pre-elementary education, with enrolments respectively of 1 per cent, vitually none, and 30 per cent. Ontario's percentage enrolment, in contrast, is particularly high at 69 per cent, since its program applies to many four-year-olds as well as to older pre-schoolers. Generally, however, enrolments in the provinces tend toward the 50 per cent mark, leaving substantial opportunities for more pre-school programming. Potential students in the four- to five-year age group, certainly not the only pre-school eligible for education, number as many as 88,000 in Quebec, 74,000 in Ontario, 42,000 in Alberta, 34,000 in British Columbia, 23,000 in New Brunswick, and several thousand in each of the remaining provinces. In Canada overall, about 321,000 children stand to gain from the development of pre-school education for four- and five-year-olds, enough to employ, for example, all Canada's redundant teachers.

Table 8

Pre-school populations and enrolments by province, 1977-1978 term

	Population aged 4 and 5 years*	Public pre-school enrolments	Enrolments as % of population aged 4-5 years
Newfoundland	23140	12380	54%
Prince Edward Island	3815	35	1
Nova Scotia	26070	14288	55
New Brunswick	23130	53	—
Quebec	171745	83970	49
Ontario	240755	166398	69
Manitoba	32590	16508	51
Saskatchewan	29660	14140	48
Alberta	60180	17971	30
British Columbia	68720	34296	50
Yukon	825	388	47
Northwest Territories	2140	1111	52
Canada:	**682790**	**361538**	**53**

*Population aged 4 and 5 years for 1978 based on 1976 Census data for population aged 2 and 3 years, ignoring deaths, migration, and immigration, while pre-school enrolments are for 1977-78 school year.
Source: Statistics Canada, *Elementary and Secondary School Enrolments*, Cat. No. 81-210, and 1976 Census.

The need for professional development

The strengthening of teachers' skills and the broadening of their knowledge are critical elements in any strategy to maintain high standards of educational quality. But particularly important in recent months and in many school districts, is their application to the problem of redundancy and uneven distribution of the teacher force. If the specialist is to become more versatile, the aging educator more current, the new recruit more secure, and the surplus teacher more useful, a wide-ranging program of professional development, additional to present upgrading efforts, should be considered.

Yet, a commitment to professional development appears lacking in Canada, a condition worsened by teacher redundancy. Arthur Schwartz, in a study of declining enrolments in British Columbia, has said: "The idea that teacher education must become continuing education in order that the effectiveness of the teaching force be maintained has not yet come into its time in this province."[20] Despite the increases in off-campus course offerings by British Columbia's faculties of education, many of the one-quarter of the province's full-time teachers who were without degrees in 1977 were unable to gain access to part-time university credit courses during the school year, according to Schwartz.

British Columbia is not unique. It its brief to the CODE in 1977, the Ontario Public School Men Teachers' Federation noted that children are not being educated adequately in many areas and that there is good reason to retrain professional staff. According to Statistics Canada, as many as 23 per cent of Canadian teachers have fewer than three university courses related to the subject they teach most often. And a 1979 Canadian Education Association survey of 245 Canadian school boards shows that 106 of them, or 43 per cent, are not engaged in "programs for upgrading or expanding teachers' qualifications".

Many teachers in Canada do not hold university degrees. According to Table 9, below, Alberta had in 1978-79 the greatest proportion of teachers with parchments (89.6 per cent), while Nova Scotia had the fewest (59.2 per cent). The discrepancy among provincial standings would lessen, however, and the actual percentages would rise if vocational

---

[20] Arthur M. Schwartz and Patrick McGowan, *Declining Enrolment: Implications for British Columbia's Public School System* (1977), p. 36.

teachers, who do not always hold degrees, yet who are put through a degree program in Alberta, were excluded from the calculation, and if graduates from Nova Scotia's non-university teacher training program were included. The picture would improve further if those teachers who are working on degrees and stand to earn them imminently were counted.

Table 9

Percentage of Canadian teachers with university degrees, selected years, 1960-78[a]

	1960-61	1964-65	1969-70	1974-75	1977-78	1978-79
Newfoundland	10.7	13.3	26.3	56.1	66.0	69.0
Prince Edward Island	7.2	11.3	24.6	48.2	62.4	65.7
Nova Scotia	23.8	28.3	39.1	52.4	57.4	59.2
New Brunswick	14.1	18.7	32.9	57.4	72.8	77.1
Ontario	27.4	32.6	-[b]	57.9	68.2	68.6
Manitoba	25.6	28.3	37.7	64.8	76.7	79.7
Saskatchewan	16.7	22.8	34.0	55.6	64.4	68.0
Alberta	27.7	35.9	52.8	77.6	87.2	89.6
British Columbia	37.0	42.3	53.7	70.4	76.2	78.0
Yukon	14.6	23.5	44.7	62.6	73.5	76.9
Northwest Territories	28.1	26.2	40.8	60.7	70.0	70.6
Total:	**25.7**	**31.1**	**43.1**	**61.5**	**71.2**	**72.7**

[a]Excluding Quebec.
[b]Data unavailable.
Source: Statistics Canada, *Salaries and Qualifications of Teachers in Public Elementary and Secondary Schools*, Cat. No. 81-202.

Still, the degreed teacher force would fall short of the 100-per cent mark, and this carries implications for professional development in Canadian schools. The rapid rise over the years in the numbers of teachers holding degrees, evidenced in the Table, is one indicator of the importance of university accreditation, and indicates indirectly the need for teachers not so trained to take other action to strengthen their professional abilities, particularly in the face of severe competition for their jobs. And, according to the Canadian Teachers' Federation, there exists a general assumption that teachers should be broadly educated and intellectually mature. The variety of disciplines and sound theoretical background gained at university are deemed important in achieving this end. It is one goal of professional development to build such strengths, and the need, especially among senior teachers, is significant.

British Columbia's Schwartz suggests that more accessible undergraduate courses in education would be worthwhile in parts of that province where non-degree teachers are prominent. But, to be useful, such courses must focus on skills clearly related to the classroom. The Toronto Board of Education echoed this proviso when it said: "One of the major continuing problems will be the difficulty of reconciling the needs of a changing program with the skills of existing staff."[21] The board stressed the importance of practical policies to best serve the actual requirements of schools. At least one working paper of the CODE emphasized the formation of practical skills through the introduction of more in-service training opportunities for special educators. And a summer program, offered at the Memorial University of Newfoundland in St. John's, is stressing practical classroom skills. The course idea met wih some faculty resistance because of its "lack of academic respectability", but, according to Brother Augustus Brennan of the Roman Catholic School Board of St. John's, it is now recognized and popular. The board's emphasis on teacher upgrading has been a factor in the popularity of this methods course.

It is not only the need to strengthen the teachers' competencies in conventional subjects and procedures which warrants development courses; subject areas of recent recognition and of growing importance are placing new demands on the system for teachers trained in new fields — two principal areas of alternative education in need of staff are special education (of the handicapped, retarded, and gifted child), and adult education.

Narrowing these gaps in service can be achieved through setting new goals for professional development. The formation of training programs hinges on at least two essentials: an inventory of student needs and present teacher skills and deployment, specifying gaps and overlaps in service; and mechanisms to effect the requisite training.

Special education and professional development One student need only partly met by present teacher skills and deployment

[21] The Director of Education, unpublished report (Toronto: Board of Education for the City of Toronto, November 18, 1977), p. 17.

and which offers an opportunity to redundant teachers is that of special education.

Research has shown children with emotional disturbances and learning disabilities can fit into and benefit from a regular classroom, according to the CODE.[22] But, one important condition is teacher training and willingness to alter instruction to suit individual children. Since educators can't be expected to perform the added responsibilities unaided, the Ontario government is encouraging this integration and helping teachers adjust to the new demands of individual pupil differences. According to the CODE, regular classroom teachers need to be equipped with the skills necessary to face a variety of problems, to select materials, and to develop instruction for a wide range of student abilities. The CODE emphasizes the redundant teacher in this role:

> In an era of declining enrolments and lack of growth in the teacher population, this means in-service and retraining, rather than pre-training. Furthermore, the integration of exceptional children requires that training be extended to regular class teachers. Thus the need is virtually as large as the teacher population.[23]

The Saskatoon School Division No. 13 hold special education as one of its top priorities. Its staff development program, conducted during the day, after school, and in the evening, is devoting a special effort to techniques of educating the handicapped and slow learners, as well as to supervision, team teaching, and classroom skills. Most of the board's 1,100 teachers are involved in the program in one way or another, according to board executive assistant William Bender. Educational leave for up to one year at two-thirds salary is also available in Saskatoon. The plan attracts about 10 people a year and, in 1979-80, focussed on special education.

Similarly, in Bathurst, New Brunswick, the local school board has taken up the cause of the special student. According to board officials, a committee comprising health specialists and administrators has been formed to find ways the school system can accommodate more youngsters with learning disabilities. The board sees an opportunity here for redundant teachers, provided they can be upgraded accordingly.

In Ontario, there are unmet needs in professional development for teachers wishing to work with particular kinds of learning disabilities, to develop assessment

---

[22] Judi B. Korbrick and Carol Reich, Declining Enrolments and its Ramification for Special Education (1978).

[23] Ibid. p. 21.

techniques and educational methods, and to get involved in administration and research. At the same time, there is the worry teachers will seek specialized training only to protect their jobs, not to satisfy a professional interest, and that supervisors may use special education as a repository for unwanted teachers. But, as competition for assignments mounts, and as administrators are more able to be selective in retraining and redeployment, redundant teachers would do well to be certain of their motives before attempting a shift.

Adult education and professional development Adult education is another emerging area of instruction in Canada. According to the Canadian Teachers' Federation, some Canadian institutions are establishing diploma programs for adult educators, but the field carries vast potential for initiative.

The varied educational needs of adults suggest several challenges teachers, trained for this area, might expect to face. Generally, there is apprehension about the instructors' ability to create an atmosphere conducive to adult learning — to base instruction on the life experience of adult students, to work creatively with traditional and innovative course content, and to identify with the undereducated, the disadvantaged, and those with learning disabilities. Aware of these needs, a CODE working paper[24] suggested that every educational institution offer in-service training to enhance the skills of adult educators.

To promote the education of female adults, the working paper proposed that all educational institutions train both their administrative and instructional personnel to avoid stereotyping in their work with women. The paper also suggests that teacher training institutions and school boards should put in place pre-service and in-service training programs to prepare guidance counsellors for the particular demands of advising girls on the sexist stereotyping which may occur in the educational system.

In response to the special needs of the immigrant student, the working paper recommended that boards and faculties of education introduce continuing education and professional development courses for teachers and administrators who work with immigrant and ethnic groups. Upgrading would place importance on an understanding of the values, customs, expectations, and communication patterns of new Canadians.

---

[24] Davie, *op. cit.*

The undereducated adult also prefers some teacher qualities to others, according to a case study reviewed by the working paper. Class attendance rates were observed to improve when the teacher was not certified, had not completed college degrees, or had not been employed as a public school teacher. In another case, literacy students voiced a preference for teachers who knew the subject well, were friendly and actually listened to the students, and who worked individually with them. These students also valued counselling highly.

There are precautions those interested in adult education ought to take before shifting to that branch of education. Another working paper of the CODE[25] found high motivation among adult learners compared with children, a difference they attribute to the mandatory nature of a child's attendance at school. The researchers suggest that such discrepancies in attitude be documented and used in the professional development of part-time adult educators. In a provincial survey, the Ontario researchers found adult educators had to "offer more choice", "give them more control", "work as peers", "act as a resource person", "review fundamentals", and "give more details". The study recommended that school boards undertake an extensive survey of instructors' learning needs and incorporate the findings into professional development programs, and that faculties of education consider introducing teachers in their pre-service training to ideas, literature, and practice relating to adult learning and teaching.

Gaps in conventional subjects and reassignment

The reassignment of teachers to a new task within the educational setting they're accustomed to can take several forms, depending on the nature of the enrolment problem. An uneven distribution of students across a province may lead to adjustment of school board boundaries, busing, or to the closing of some schools and the building of others. In each case, reassignment involves moving the teacher from one region of the province to another to teach what he is already teaching.

The rolling of a peak-enrolment wave through the grades, leaving some classrooms crowded and others relatively empty in different years, may require the reassignment of teachers among grades and between elementary and secondary levels.

---

[25] James Draper and Donald Keating, *Instructors of Adults* (1978).

Teachers may have to shift among subjects as well. A combination of these problems could see teachers moving among divisions, changing grades, and specializing in new subjects.

There is more scope for reassignment than might be expected, according to Statistics Canada data. Many teachers have little or no formal university training in the subject they teach most of the time. Table 10 reveals the mismatch of training to assignment among Canadian secondary school teachers in 1977-78.

Table 10

Percentage of teachers with fewer than three university courses related to their main assignment*

	Physical sciences	Social studies	Mathematics	French	English
Percentage	15	16	23	14	12

*Excluding Ontario
Source: C.T. Curteis, Education, Science, and Culture Division, Statistics Canada, Ottawa. Unpublished paper (November 1979).

According to the federal agency, most of these teachers have a university specialty in one or more of the other academic areas. It's therefore likely that a transfer of assignment within or among schools would lessen the mismatch problem.

Random attrition and shifting educational priorities have added another dimension to the matching problem. Even though there may be surplus teachers in some subjects, there may be too few in others, and, according to school boards across the country, conventional subjects are encountering a mismatch of teacher and assignment. There is a need for more teachers in these areas:
• second languages
• guidance
• art and music
• vocations, particularly automotives, carpentry, and business education.

This deficiency sometimes manifests itself as an actual shortage requiring a transfer of teachers between schools, a common procedure at the Calgary Board of Education and at the London Board of Education where transfers among 16 secondary schools tripled between 1978 and 1979. In other cases, all positions may be filled, but the loss of a teacher during the term could mean an extended vacancy as adminstrators seek out a replacement from what Bill Blake of the Vancouver School Board describes as a "thin pool" of manpower in these areas.

Need may also be expressed as a potential shortage which could materialize in the near future, and which could be averted through retraining now. At the School Board for the Municipality of the District of Lunenburg in Bridgewater, Nova Scotia, teachers desiring professional development must first satisfy the superintendent of their proficiency in reading skills, human relations, and mathematics, current priorities at that board. Any upgrading efforts would have to remedy those shortfalls before new directions could be taken.

Saturated subjects include these:
- science
- geography
- social studies
- physical education
- history
- English

Teachers in these oversupplied areas are involved in professional development, partly as a way to meet the heavy competition for their jobs, and partly as a remedy for the problem of burn-out experienced by many teachers with advanced seniority.

A variety of mechanisms to improve the professional standing of teachers has come into being in Canada, some more favoured than others. These include:
- leave of various durations and at various proportions of salary to encourage graduate study, work study for vocational teachers, catching up on degree courses, and independent study projects
- in-service training during the day, after school, in the evening, on weekends, or during summer school, to strengthen practical skills and supervisory abilities
- self-initiated study on a teacher's own time
- teacher service on curriculum committees, and the editing or writing of textbooks
- sabbaticals to permit travel and study, retirement planning, or leisure pursuits
- exchange of teachers among boards
- international exchange

Some jurisdictions offer up to three months' leave with pay, and grant further time without remuneration. Some allow up to one year with two-thirds salary. Some place importance on curriculum committee work, others don't. In some areas, sabbaticals are common, in others, out of the question.

If boards were to reallocate their teacher manpower extensively and find they still had too many educators, the problem of oversupply would take on added importance and reassignment beyond provincial boundaries would be necessary. Teachers might move to other provinces or they might go abroad. And, there are opportunities beyond the classroom.

A program of particular interest is the Provincial Teacher Exchange Program of Ontario. The program is designed to speed the personal growth of a teacher employed by one board through exposure to the ideas, resources, programs, and staff of another board, and through sharing ideas and expertise with other students, teachers, parents, and board officials. Each board continues to pay its own teacher's salary and benefits; each appointment lasts one year.

Under the program, Bruce Black of Queen Elizabeth Collegiate and Vocational Institute in Kingston, Ontario, moved to Selkirk Collegiate in Thunder Bay for the 1979-80 school year. Bruce finds the change refreshing and his exposure to new colleagues informative, but he questions the impact that the switch will have on his professional growth. Bruce thinks a posting at a school strikingly different from that which a teacher is used to would offer a variety of experience. But the environment at his new school is so similar to that of Queen Elizabeth that Bruce doesn't expect a radical broadening of his professional horizons.

Looking to teacher mobility beyond national boundaries, the Ontario Teachers' Federation has decided to commit $50,000 to finding employment for its members overseas. The sum allocated to teacher placement will permit the federation to enter the market for international education contracts and effectively export Canadian teachers to countries needing skilled educators. (A complementary plan would see the encouragement of foreign students to attend schools in Canada.) Reassigned in this way, Ontario's teachers will remain in the education field, expand their skills, and be in a position to return to Ontario when enrolments warrant it. The federation is exploring the formation of a non-profit corporation involving all levels of the educational system to administer the program.

According to the Organisation for Economic Co-operation and Development, the 35th session of the International

Conference on Education, held August 27 to September 4, 1975, in Geneva, predicted an increase in the teacher requirements of developing countries until 1985. The OECD sees considerable opportunity in these countries for redundant teachers:

> The developing countries' own resources are not sufficient to meet these requirements. The surplus situation prevailing in a number of developed countries might allow them to consider sending more of their qualified manpower, especially teaching staff, to these countries in the general framework of national or international assistance.[26]

The Protestant School Board of Greater Montreal also has endorsed the idea of overseas service for Canadian teachers. In an address to a conference on redundancy in Ottawa in November 1979, hosted by the Canadian Education Association, the board's director general, Marcel Fox, drew attention to the advantages of foreign postings:

> The programs of assistance to underdeveloped countries are widespread but mostly concern business and industry rather than education. It would be wise and helpful if the possibilities of sending trained, experienced teachers abroad for a certain period of time, were taken into consideration. Such teachers, well versed in their subject, would be able to help their colleagues overseas and would at the same time acquire new knowledge, new experience and a new appreciation of their own society. At the same time, these well selected emissaries would enhance Canada's image on an international level.[27]

A further advantage is, of course, the reduction of domestic teacher supply without a permanent loss of qualified personnel.

Keeping teachers in the country, but assigning them outside the classroom, is another option for educational decision-makers. Colleges, universities, and employers have been known to criticize the language ability of post-secondary students and graduates. Professors spend inordinate amounts of their time on the basics of composition and grammar. Employers must hire remedial writing consultants to raise the standards of written communication in their organizations. Mr. Fox has suggested assigning teachers to these institutions for one year periods to assess and to improve students' essays. Such a theme would free up professors' time and would give secondary teachers the opportunity to gauge the weaknesses of students who have recently left the secondary classroom.

* * *

---

[26] Organisation for Economic Co-operation and Development, *Teacher Policies in a New Context* (1979), p. 58.

[27] Marcel R. Fox, *Positive Strategies for Retraining* (1979), p. 9.

Where a mismatch of teacher to assignment, only one dimension of redundancy, is the central problem confronting boards, systematic reassignment of educators presents a complete and long-term solution. Where redundancy is more serious and no shuffling of personnel can alleviate completely excess supply, inter-provincial migration of teachers and overseas placement will offer relief, but, like part-time teaching, the advantages are temporary. Only so many people are willing to move away from their homes; and they probably view the relocation as short-term; in time, they will be among the many seeking urban employment. And exported teachers are bound to return.

Administrative roles and professional development

As well as strengthening teacher skills, professional development can foster advancement of educators to administrative positions. Management of the educational system during contraction, even during stability, should prove a more onerous task than administering growth — in the same way that bad news is more awkward to convey than good. Decisions will be negative and problems of equity and morale will test the imagination of supervisors and administrators to new limits. So, new people with new talents would be an asset in senior posts.

Arthur Schwartz put the case this way:

It is administrative and supervisory personnel who will bear the burden of directing their districts' responses to decline; their abilities to do so creatively, rather than attempting to force past procedures and solutions to fit today's and tomorrow's problems, will be the key to maintaining the quality of education in the districts so affected.[28]

Adding to the need for professional development posed by the demand of managing contraction is the tendency for shrinking divisions to drive out promising young talent as they cut back administrative staff at the very time they need it most. The implication is clear, according to Schwartz:

Shrinking districts, especially the smaller ones, may thus face the prospects not only of reduced or eliminated input of fresh personnel, but also of losing their most promising and capable young staff members, as bright and ambitious teachers and junior administrators move to those districts which offer better chances of promotion . . .

Such an eventuality will pose serious difficulties for the districts affected, since the demands for insightful and creative leadership will

---

[28] Schwartz, *op. cit.* p. 37.

*be considerable in times of decline. Districts will need effective
leadership, and they will have to provide incentives for their more
capable and ambitious staff in order to keep them while at the same
time operating under financial constraints.*[29]

Manitoba's Lord Selkirk School Division has proposed one
such incentive. Concerned with strengthening teachers'
leadership potential, the division expects to introduce an
"internship program" in 1980. Under the purview of the
superintendent's department, the Manitoba Teachers' Society,
principals, and the school board, a principal and his "intern"
would embark upon 20 days of school or division office work
spread over the year. The teacher would gain first-hand
knowledge of budgeting, scheduling, curriculum development,
staff development, program evaluation, and supervisory roles.
One-half of the training time would be arranged through
release from assignment, with the balance comprising
weekend or holiday hours.

A progression of the plan would have a teacher replace his
principal for a short time, assuming responsibility for the
operation of the school while the principal pursues
development of his own, involves himself in division policy
work, or takes a leave of absence.

The division foresees these advantages to the program:
• development of a pool of talent for potential leadership
• improvement of present administrators through their
instructional role in the program and through release for study
• creation of an outlet for aspiring staff
• rejuvenation of mid-career administrators

The division has estimated the cost per trainee to be $530
plus the time devoted by principals and central administration
staff to the process.

* * *

Because the "redundancy" problem is as much a matter of too
few dollars as of too many teachers, goverments are unlikely to
spend freely to prepare teachers for redirection within their
profession, despite defensible education needs. But if there are
shortages governments are committed to eliminate, or
alternative education they are prepared to fund, it will likely
prove cheaper to reallocate teachers already in the work force
than to produce new graduates at around $14,000 each to fill
the gaps.

If those graduates already exist and they are without work,

[29] *Ibid.*, p. 38.

however, then thrifty administrators will prefer engaging them at a lower starting salary to paying experienced teachers advanced sums to do the same work. The opportunities that shortages present to the redundant teacher willing to be retrained and reassigned, therefore, depend on the existence of a ready or imminent stock of graduates capable of filling the open positions. If faculties and their students have misjudged market needs and money availability to the extent school boards have, the redundant teacher can look with some hope to the professional development option.

So, on-the-job improvement is a choice for the redundant teacher only where geographic dispersion of teachers is uneven, where boards are short manpower in some subjects, where a commitment exists to expand special and adult education, where the requisite knowledge can be gained in the short term, and where new graduates are insufficient to meet the market. It isn't a remedy for redundancy *per se*. If these conditions do not exist, teacher development certainly remains an important route to improving the quality of education, but is becomes merely "academic" as a solution to the surplus educator.

Chapter 5
Rerouting redundant teachers out of teaching

The practicality of part-time teaching, or the opportunity for the betterment of vocational skills offered by professional development, will certainly find favour among some educators. Those teachers prepared to weather the storm of a glut on the market for their services, those interested in strengthening their versatility, or those willing to work fewer hours, yet keep their jobs and benefits, will see the appeal of such strategies.

But for others, the threat or the reality of unemployment will prove a strong incentive to seek out work in a field less plagued by uncertainty, yet one where the skills still apply. This preference will exist despite claims that redundancy will vanish in a few years, giving way, in fact, to a shortage of teachers in Canadian schools, even in Ontario schools. There are choices for these teachers as well. Extended leave, permitting the teacher to work in a new field for a time, travel, or just relax, is made possible through deferred income plans and leave-without-pay arrangements. Early retirement can solve a variety of problems. Career workshops, in preparation for an actual change of jobs can be invaluable to the redundant teacher. Dismissal is the last resort for the over-staffed school board, and one which has brewed controversy as different jurisdictions use different approaches in exercising this option.

Deferred income plans

Deferring a portion of salary for four years, then taking a "paid" leave of absence for one year, financed with that delayed income, is a plan gaining in popularity in Canada. The forced-saving scheme not only gives teachers the chance to try out or train for a new field, or take an extended holiday, but helps obviate dismissal and opens up teaching jobs.

At the Lakehead Board of Education, the "four-five" plan works this way. In each of four years, the board pays a teacher a reduced salary. The unpaid amount is banked and accrues to the teacher in the fifth year of the plan, the year he is on leave. The deducted salary earns interest, calculated monthly and determined by averaging the interest rates in effect on the last day of each month for a true savings account, a one-year term deposit, a three-year term deposit, and a five-year term deposit. During the four years, benefits tied to salary remain unchanged, and, in the year of leave, benefits paid are based on the teacher's salary in the fourth year. Fringe benefits continue during the fifth year, but the employee pays the premium costs.

Only teachers with three years' service to the board are eligible to participate in the plan, and anyone who has taken a prior leave without fulfilling all the requirements thereof is ineligible. Upon return from his year off, the teacher is entitled to assume his original position with the board unless a change in enrolment has made the post unnecessary; settlement of that issue requires reference to the collective agreement. Should a teacher enrolled in the plan be deemed redundant and ineligible to return to the board for one full year beyond the year of his planned leave, he must withdraw from the plan. In that event, the teacher receives the money he has paid into the plan, plus interest earned.

Teachers may withdraw from the plan any time prior to March 1 of the calendar year in which the leave is to begin; his savings and interest are refunded. Where the board cannot find a suitable replacement for the leaving teacher, it may defer the year off, giving the teacher the option of remaining in the plan or withdrawing the funds owing him.

A drawback of the Lakehead plan — the four-year delay of the leave — has been avoided in some other plans, among them the Vernon, British Columbia, school district program, and the plan at the Board of Education for the City of London. In Vernon, teachers work the first two years of the five-year program, then are eligible for leave, thanks to a general fund used to finance the earlier absence. In London, teachers may leave as early as the second year. To finance the absence in years two, three, or four, all teachers pay $25 from each pay cheque into a trust fund administered by their board. That fund finances a teacher's leave if it occurs before year five, and, when he returns, the board continues deducting part of his salary for the remaining years of his subscription to the plan to replenish the account. Essentially, then, Ontario secondary school teachers are extending a loan to those among them who haven't banked enough for their leave but wish to take a year off.

According to the Niagara South Board of Education, the principal benefit of such plans to the individual is that the board acts as a financial manager for a substantial portion of the teacher's savings and finances a part of the leave by allowing it to be taken before the teacher has made a full contribution. And, according to investment analysts, it can be a good idea for a teacher to hand over responsibility for deducting and saving the money to someone else. Regular deductions are less painful, and the temptation of withdrawing the funds and spending them is not nearly so strong as it would be in a personal savings account.

Already, 50 teachers have signed up for the London plan. The first eight are due to leave in 1980-81. The plan expires in 1984.

Leave without pay

There was a time leave without pay was beyond the reach of many teachers. Today, boards are easing the criteria for time off, and many more teachers are availing themselves of the chance for a diversion from the classroom. George Bolivar of Newcombville, Nova Scotia, is such a teacher.

The 21-year veteran of high school science teaching in Nova Scotia left his job two years ago to try residential general contracting. His position and seniority with the school board were guaranteed. After a year, George found he needed more time to be sure the business would thrive, so he arranged one more year off. If he decides not to return to teaching this fall, he will forfeit his position. But he is exploring the possiblity of returning to teaching for a year, and taking leave again. He has found the experience invaluable.

"You can get into a rut in teaching and you can't get out. The experience you gain through leave would be valuable in the classroom...I think all teachers should have to take a year off and get into something else."

Apart from its advantages to the individual, leave without pay allows a board either to keep the teacher's position vacant, or to fill the post with a less costly educator, offering experience, for example, to a new graduate.

Career workshops

Anxious to change with the times, rather than fall prey to them, many teachers are taking the necessary steps to switch careers. Reaching the decision to abandon classroom teaching, probably the least savoury move in a career shift, is by no means the only hurdle to be crossed. Armed with the conviction their skills can be of value elsewhere, teachers still must learn the techniques of the job search, determine their strengths and weaknesses, then find suitable employment with a sufficient income.

School boards, particularly in Ontario, are aiding this process by sponsoring workshops on the range of skills and procedures essential to a successful job hunt. Last year, the Ottawa Board of Education organized a two-day workshop for 16 of its 176 teachers facing unemployment that fall. Seminar leader Bob George of Lalonde-George Job Hunting Co. advised the teachers on arranging interviews over the telephone, dressing for a job interview, getting past receptionists, and writing a better resume.

In Metropolitan Toronto, the Ontario Secondary School Teachers' Federation, expecting 5,000 secondary teaching posts to disappear over the next seven years, hired a computer-based personnel selection firm to screen and place teachers in new jobs. Peter Donnelly and Associates Ltd. of Toronto offers 24 hours of counselling designed to help teachers sell themselves in the labour market through appealing resumes, convincing covering letters, and creating a favourable impression during interviews. Then, the firm draws up personality and skills profiles of teachers, attempting to match these to profiles of job possibilities. Fields with the most potential, according to the placement firm, were real estate and insurance companies in need of salespeople. The teachers' federation pays the $15,000 cost of the program.

At the North York board, a series of career workshops each spring helps prepare teachers for a change. Begun in 1978, the sessions have proven successful as a source of motivation, according to the board. Teacher employability has been surprising, and several firms have actually contacted the board regularly to ask for their latest list of surplus teachers.

In June 1978, Ontario's Etobicoke Board of Education, following the lead of the North York board, offered redundant teachers a series of eight-hour workshops designed to build self-confidence and improve a teacher's ability to market himself. Co-sponsors included the Women Teachers' Association of Etobicoke, the Ontario Public School Men Teachers' Federation, and the Ontario Secondary School Teachers' Federation. Areas of employment suggested by seminar leader and management consultant Sherle Perkins-Vasey included editing, writing, and sales representative positions with publishers, particularly of school textbooks. Teachers can expect to spend at least six months looking for new jobs comparable in challenge and salary to teaching. According to the board, the seminars have been successful; placement has been easy and new employers pleased.

At Montreal's Dawson College, a course is available to teachers contemplating a new career. Concerned with developing individuals' awareness of their transferable skills, broadening their knowledge of occupations beyond teaching, and actually finding reasonable alternatives for teachers, the course draws upon a career planning guide entitled, *Teachers Without Classrooms*, published by the Guidance Centre, Faculty of Education, University of Toronto. The booklet offers a particularly realistic view of the career change process. It puts the stress on the need to know what a new employer expects and the ability to adapt to new demands.

Once outside the education field the teacher may have to become accustomed to more frequent criticism. In education, evaluation is usually very formal and very supportive. If it is necessary to reprimand a teacher the matter is usually delicately handled. In business and industry, immediate supervisors may be extremely critical of a person's performance without considering advance notice, without putting the criticism in writing, and with full knowledge that the individual has no recourse. Thus, "power" is a concept to cope with as the teacher moves into a business environment: how to get it and how to use it.[30]

An individual may be more closely supervised outside teaching, according to the pamphlet. While a teacher on permanent contract may have little day-to-day supervision

---

[30] John T. Price and Larry M. Cash, *Teachers Without Classrooms, A Career Planning Guide for Teachers Leaving the Profession* (1979), p. 5.

and few, if any, formal evaluations, in business and government, appraisals are routine and frequent. Employee assessments occur two or three times a year, and, in some cases, every month.

And the newcomer may have to become more accommodating in his relationships with clients. Although the teacher can be said to enjoy a certain power advantage when dealing with students, and, to a lesser extent, with parents, his role in sales, for example, can be markedly more servile. An undesirable student may fail, with little reflection on the teacher's ability or attitude. But a dissatisfied customer need simply take his business elsewhere, and the inflexible employee may be dismissed.

Teachers in a new work environment may need to become more aggressively competitive, says the planning guide. Many positions in the private sector do not offer automatic annual increments or permanent contracts. In these instances, success can depend heavily on one's ambition, determination, and resourcefulness.

Because productivity in education is highly intangible, teachers will have to pay particular attention to output in their new careers. As educators, they were judged largely on their input — their qualifications, attitude, contribution to the life of the school, implementation of curriculum. In the private business sector, input may not matter at all; many jobs pay on productivity, with volume of sales or numbers of new contracts the determinants of pay hikes and bonuses.

The booklet also reminds teachers they could well have to expect working in several capacities before finding exactly what they like or what they're good at. Time available for socializing or for family responsibilities during this period may be severely limited. Careers teachers have entered with noticeable ease include staff training and development, sales representative positions in educational, medical, computer, technical, and sales fields, real estate sales, marketing research and analysis, insurance investigation and adjustment, public relations, and a variety of occupations in the federal and provincial civil service. *Teachers Without Classrooms* outlines career possibilities according to a teacher's specialty in the manner presented in Table 11 (p. 70).

Armed with the advice of the *Teachers Without Classrooms* booklet, and with the practical guidance of career workshops, teachers are setting out to refute the unflattering adage that "those who can, do; those who can't, teach". And teachers willing to return to their profession once the market loosens will be the better for it, it's claimed, because of their exposure to discipline, scrutiny, and the need to apply their knowledge, not just convey it.

Table 11

Teacher career possibilities according to subject specialty or degree major

Subject specialty or degree major	Career possibility
1. English, history, geography, psychology, guidance, sociology, languages:	Lawyer, reporter, political analyst, advertising writer, author, police officer, social worker, community planner, personnel worker, translator.
2. Art, music, theatre arts, library sciences, family studies:	Radio and television programming, performing arts, commercial design artist, arts critic, archivist, museum worker, nutritionist, interior designer.
3. Biology, chemistry, physics, geology, mathematics, physical education:	Researcher, biologist, chemist, dentist, physician, pharmacist, laboratory technologist, nurse, surveyor, statistician, actuary, engineer, physiologist, health consultant.
4. Accounting, marketing, data processing, secretarial science:	Internal auditor, accountant, purchasing agent, business systems analyst, computer programmer, executive secretary, banker.
5. Technical education:	Technical writer, technician/technologist, industrial safety inspector, tradesman.

Source: John T. Price and Larry Cash, Teachers Without Classrooms, A Career Planning Guide for Teachers Leaving the Profession (Toronto: Guidance Centre, Faculty of Education, University of Toronto, 1979).

Early retirement

A growing preference for leisure time in Canada over the last two decades is leading more and more people to an early retirement. For those seeking a shorter working life, the road out is smoother thanks to an employers' interest in making room for younger talent, and to organizations that advise prospective retirees on the preparation an early retirement requires. But an opposing and more recent force, economic strife, is encouraging workers to hold on to what they've got. Only time will reveal the dominant trend.

However, in education, the pattern is clear. The teacher force in Canada is aging as educators hold on to their positions longer, and move among boards less, aware of the uncertainty in their profession. So school boards are finding they must make a special effort to aid advance retirement as one strategy to gain a better foothold in their struggle with excess staff.

At the Lakehead Board, an early retirement incentive plan is prompting secondary teachers over 55 with at least 10 years' service to the board to retire early. One pitfall of early retirement — the reduction of pension earnings which are based on salary prior to retirement — is overcome in part by the Lakehead scheme. During each year of participation in the early retirement incentive plan, the teacher agrees to work for the board on a mutually-agreed upon assignment for 20 days at $250 a day. According to the board, "The plan will provide the teacher with an opportunity to earn money following retirement, which will help reduce the impact of any penalties incurred under the terms of the Superannuation Act by retiring early."

In Quebec, early retirement can be particularly attractive. A teacher with 34 years' service can retire one year early, yet receive his normal salary for that year and regular superannuation thereafter, provided his departure opens a job to another teacher. The Montreal Catholic School Commission reports about 10 teachers a year in the English sector alone choosing the pre-retirement option. In the French sector, about 60 teachers took advantage of the plan in 1979-80.

Early retirement poses a longer-term solution to redundancy than such options as part-time teaching or professional development. The reduction in staff can be sure to occur every year as earlier retirement ages are reached sooner and teachers leave, opening positions for younger teachers or simply avoiding the need for dismissal. And the reduction in staff is permanent.

Dismissal

Redundant teachers have been fired at several boards across the country. Although dismissal is a choice for the school board facing redundancy, and although it does offer a long-term remedy to the problem of too many teachers, it remains an unsavoury solution and one which must be approached with caution.

Probationary teachers are usually the first to go. Then, in most districts, permanent staff are dismissed, based on their seniority, and, to a lesser extent, on program needs. Seniority is a relatively simple dismissal criterion for administrators to enforce, and is the preferred standard of most unions, but there is still disagreement on its suitability.

Faculty of education staff and students have an interest in the use of qualifications and performance as the determinant of a teacher's future, for these are the requirements that would give them a reasonably competitive chance at a teaching job. Younger members of teachers' federations also favour these standards because many of them hold probationary or part-time appointments and stand to gain little in the short-term from the protection of seniority. Boards, although acknowledging the convenience of the years-of-service criterion, are apprehensive of the long-term impact on the quality of education of letting only the younger, and possibly better educated and more highly motivated, teachers go or fail in their efforts to enter the system and retaining the older ones who may not necessarily be better educators. Teachers with several years' service to their credit — a sizable portion of the teacher force — favour the security of seniority protection.

The Federation of Women Teachers' Associations of Ontario, and the Ontario Public School Men Teachers' Federation have agreed that "a teacher's redundancy may be determined on the basis of seniority within the employed group covered by the collective agreement", and that "neither merit nor qualifications be used in the determination of redundancy".[31] In the event that two teachers hold equal service to a board, yet one of them must go, the federations propose this set of criteria in this order for making the final determination:
- length of total employment as an elementary teacher with the board and its predecessors
- length of total employment as a teacher with the board and its predecessors

[31] "Joint Redundancy Policy in Place," *Ontario Public School Men Teachers' Federation News*, 1 June, 1979, p. 4.

- length of total employment as an elementary teacher in Ontario
- length of total employment as a teacher in Ontario
- length of total employment as a teacher in Canada
- by lot

Some on the management side disagree, among them the Manitoba Association of School Trustees, which has said: "Trustees believe that the process of educating children is vastly different from, and more important than, an assembly line. Retention of teachers on the basis of seniority may bear no relationship to the best interests of students."[32]

Yet, board officials deciding the fate of teachers in overstaffed schools are doomed to face their own version of Catch 22. If surplus teachers are to be selected justly, then some set of criteria, including talent, will inevitably come into play. But, however fair this formula may seem, appealing to that abiding faith in merit as the decider of one's fate, there remains concern over staff evaluation becoming a tool solely of the redundancy hunt rather than of the standards-setting process generally. If evaluation is seen to be an upstart policy in the wake of declining enrolments, then the suggestion will be clear that staff assessment is not a regular part of education's personnel policy, and that to be redundant is to be incompetent. Painted with this brush, teachers dismissed will be lucky to find work at all.

On the other hand, if it is assumed that evaluation is a long standing and integral part of board administration, and that no school board employs deficient teachers, then a competence measure itself becomes redundant. And if one rejects tenure and seniority as reactionary ways of deciding who stays and who goes, little more than the two sides of a coin remain at the disposal of the axeman.

---

[32] "Lay-off to Court," *MAST Newsletter*, 15 April 1979, p. 4.

Chapter 6

Financing the solutions

The widely held belief that everyone should contribute to education budgets because everyone, not just those receiving the education, benefits from it, holds important implications not only for the employment of teachers but for their re-education as well. That belief has manifested itself in free primary and secondary education, where facilities have been built and staff paid out of tax revenues, and in cheap post-secondary education, be it technical training or university or continuing education, where a considerable portion of costs is paid out of public funds.

That belief has also manifested itself in the training policies of employers, and these can be valuable benchmarks in any consideration of teacher re-education. Often, employees receive in-service training free, and further education at little or no cost. On the reasoning that a better educated employee improves the earning capacity of the firm, companies guarantee an employee's job during an extended educational leave, pay some or all of his salary while he's gone, and cover his various expenses.

Governments can be particularly generous in educating their own employees, perhaps following the logic behind their very existence — that the public, not the individual, should finance certain activities, including education, because the public benefits. Some governments offer extensive retraining benefits to employees, including paid overseas education, free cross-Canada learning tours, and elaborate educational leaves.

Governments' belief in the social benefits of education also carries into their other job market activities. The job-finding service of federal employment centres is offered at no charge. Revenue Canada permits taxpayers to deduct from their taxable income money spent on education. And, the expense of moving closer to one's job can be a deduction against the tax bite.

But it's not only for education and retraining where workers have enjoyed subsidies of one sort or another. Transfers are an expense employers almost always finance. In the private sector, employees wishing to move across or up the hierarchy are given the necessary funds. And it is common for redundant employees to be relocated at company expense, but usually only if the the firm has offices in another city.

The cost to an employee of dismissal — lost earnings for a period of time and damage to long-term earning prospects — is often covered by the employer, even if the discharge follows from employee redundancy. Severance pay is common in Canada, its advantages especially welcome when a worker faces few other choices of work. Even resignations, for whatever reason, have been known to earn the leaving employee severance pay.

So, just as the philosophy of public education leaves no doubt about how or why teachers are paid for their time, it also carries important implications for teacher retraining and for general teacher welfare. Labour practices in other sectors offer guidelines for the treatment of teachers, whether in their professional development, dismissal, their choice of a new career, or in the expansion of the market for their labour.

Financing professional development and reassignment

Economists have demonstrated the contribution education can make to income and to economic growth generally. It is on these grounds that governments have introduced what Milton Friedman[33] calls an "indiscriminate extension" of their responsibility into formal schooling.

[33] Milton Friedman, *Capitalism and Freedom*, (1962).

Some observers admit gains from schooling may be overestimated, largely because the contribution of other factors to an individual's growth, principally on-the-job training, has been overlooked. The apparent value of such job-related learning is prompting employers to allocate considerable sums to this pursuit. And whether Friedman would term these expenditures indiscriminate too has not hampered their permeation of business and government on a wide scale.

Examples of retraining and reassignment philosophies and practices in business and government abound, only some of which are parallelled in the education sector.

The Bank of Montreal, for example, encourages employees to take a series of night courses developed jointly by the Institute of Canadian Bankers and the University of Toronto. The bank pays all expenses, and offers an honorarium which can total $1,100 depending on the number of courses successfully completed. Employees attending degree programs can expect financial assistance from the bank, depending on the relevance of the instruction to their professional responsibilities, and they enjoy job security as well. If an employee must move within the bank's network of branches, all costs are paid.

Canadian Pacific offers internal short courses in management, supervision, and sales at no cost to the employee. Attendance at the Banff School of Advanced Management and the University of Western Ontario for a few weeks is a company-financed benefit. And, employees taking longer leave are assisted with their expenses and are sure of a job when they return. Transfers anywhere in Canada are paid.

The Manitoba Civil Service Commission offers the usual array of internal instruction and short-term external courses. Additionally, the government will offer up to full pay to an employee on extended educational leave if the training is employer-initiated. For employee-initiated course work, the government will pay one-half of the expenses upon successful completion of the course, and offers a monthly allowance of up to $490. In the event of a move, all employee relocation expenses are paid as well. The government is also considering the idea of a short-term student-civil servant swap as a way to advance the education of employees and offer practical experience to students.

The federal government administers similar programs for the improvement of employee skills, but some of its advanced management courses are particularly interesting.

An employee with five years' experience with the Canadian government and a sound record of achievement can be eligible for a 13-month management course which embodies, among other learning experiences, a cross-Canada tour. Full salary is paid and job security guaranteed. The Public Service Commission also offers special development courses in Europe, designed mainly for staff in external affairs, immigration, industry and commerce, and the Export Development Corporation. Out-of-pocket expenses, travel costs, charges for the storage of personal effects, and salary are paid. The trainee is assured a job at least equal to that which he left, and there is no return service requirement, a common obligation of provincial governments concerned with losing their investment should the trainee resign upon returning. Ottawa describes the commitment as a "gentlemen's agreement".

Federal civil servants planning a move within the government can count on their employer paying not only all moving expenses, often including real estate fees, but also funding for a "house hunting" trip in advance of the actual move.

The field of nursing relies on several sources of funding for its professional development. According to the Saskatchewan Registered Nurses' Association, the province's College of Nursing administers a Continuing Nursing Education Program, partly funded through tuition fees and partly by the college's own resources. The Saskatchewan Union of Nurses also pays for some professional development, and the association itself grants about $10,000 a year in bursary money. The Victorian Order of Nurses extends a bursary as well to worthy applicants, and the provincial government promotes the study of public health through a bursary program. Hospitals, as the employer of nurses, of course help cover some of the expense of continuing education. And, such non-profit organizations as the Tuberculosis Association and the Heart Fund extend financial assistance for study in their areas.

An innovative source of funding for professional development has emerged from the federal Adams Commission on educational leave and productivity. Rejecting government-subsidized training as ineffective, the report places the responsibility for vocational training on employers, recommending that a training levy be applied throughout Canadian industry.

The levy would equal the total expenditure on vocational

training required of employers, thus employers should be able to write off against the levy their costs of routine apprenticeship training and other programs leading to improved occupational qualifications. The commission has proposed, however, that only programs that lead to actual certificates, diplomas, or degrees should qualify for credit.

The commission feels a levy of 0.5 per cent of payroll would meet conventional standards, and would save the federal government a considerable sum as it was able to contract or eliminate its various training subsidy programs. The commission would, in turn, remit this saving to industry as a tax deduction, reducing the firms' tax liability by more than the amount they spend on training, provided they spend the full amount required. Companies not spending the prescribed proportion of payroll would have to pay the unspent moneys to the government.

Financing dismissal

Redundancy is by no means unique to the teaching profession; it first became evident as an economic reality in the mining operations of West Virginia, Nova Scotia, and Wales. There, workers were displaced by technology. In other cases, they lost their jobs because their skills became obsolete or because demand dried up — the case in the teaching profession. Since its recognition, such structural unemployment has been largely confined to industry, particularly heavy manufacturing. Teacher redundancy is only a recent phenomenon and probably a temporary one, but teachers do stand to learn from the experience of industry in coping with obsolescence and dismissal.

When Winnipeg's Swift meat packing plant closed in 1979, the firm let 500 people go. Employees with 10 years' service received 7½ weeks' severance pay and 1½ weeks' pay for every additional year. Those few employees the firm was able to retain for its offices elsewhere received full compensation for their moving expenses and costs of selling their homes.

Concerned with that kind of possibility in their field, the United Auto Workers have negotiated a "supplementary unemployment benefits plan" with the major automobile makers. Under the plan, the employer pays into a benefits fund until it reaches a specified limit. Then, in the event of a model change lay-off or a more serious shutdown, the fund supplements the employees' unemployment insurance benefits to ensure their earnings equal 95 per cent of the net income they were receiving. Workers with one year's experience are eligible to draw, and payments are made for up to a year.

The plan is effective for lay-offs of about a year's duration. Thereafter, it begins to fail as the fund dwindles and eventually goes broke. This tendency, ironically, harms the workers with the most seniority: because senior employees are always the last to go, the account is exhausted by the time they are eligible for its benefits. When Chrysler of Canada began discharging 3,000 workers in the spring of 1979, its supplementary benefits fund started to diminish; by September it had vanished.

When Inco laid off 1,800 employees in February 1978, at its Sudbury operation, the only money to change hands was holiday pay, according to the union. Since then, the United Steel Workers of America Local 6500 has negotiated a supplementary benefits scheme similar to that of the auto workers. When the fund reaches $3.7 million, any laid-off employee receives up to $40 a week as a supplement to unemployment insurance payments for up to one year. Another part of the collective agreement stipulates preferential recall of laid-off employees for up to 24 months after dismissal.

When the Progressive Conservative government of Manitoba dismissed 100 permanent and 200 term employees in March 1978 as part of the administration's restraint program, up to six weeks' pay was extended as severance allowance. Senior officer employees received one month's salary for each year they had been with the government, to a maximum of three months' pay.

If a federal civil servant in the education bargaining group were to face dismissal, he would be assured two weeks' severance pay for his first year of service, and one week's pay for each succeeding complete year of continuous employment, to a maximum of 28 weeks. Should the employee rejoin the civil service and encounter a second lay-off, he would receive one week for each year, less the previous severance pay, to a maximum of 27 weeks. Partial years are rounded down.

A federal civil servant who resigns after ten years' service is entitled to severance pay equal to one-half his weekly rate of pay times his number of completed years to a maximum of 26 years.

Severance pay for teachers is uncommon in Canada, and the generosity of settlements varies. In one case, four days' pay was offered for each year of service, to a maximum of 140 days, and, in another, five days' pay. In one case in Nova Scotia, 40 per cent of salary was paid only if employees had five years' service; those with fewer years' service received nothing. And, in a settlement in Nipissing, teachers with one year's experience received 10 per cent of their salary; those with more service received more, to a maximum of 50 per cent for nine years' service.

The Lakehead board, acutely aware of the redundancy problem, will pay surplus teachers about a third of their salary. And, in a variation of severance pay, the board offers teachers who voluntarily choose to resign a lump sum based on the employee's accumulated sick days and annual salary. The formula results in several thousand dollars accruing to teachers who leave.

In Quebec, surplus teachers who find another job may receive up to six months' salary as a severance allowance, provided the resignation creates a job for another teacher.

Financing transition to a new career

The cost of shifting to a new career may vary depending on the nature of the individual's current job and the policies of his future employer. In business and government, interview trips are common, with the prospective employer financing interviewees' travel to the site of the interview. Depending on the individual's certainty about the new job, the paid trip may also give him the chance to check the housing market in the new locale. Such arrangements are virtually unknown in the teaching field.

Teachers can benefit, however, from Canada Employment centres' job-finding services, advice on job interview techniques, and possible financial aid for job hunting and relocation. And in Ontario, the province with the most serious teacher redundancy problem in Canada, several organizations are sponsoring workshops and seminars on the special problem of finding suitable employment for displaced educators.

The Etobicoke Board of Education, in conjunction with the Women Teachers' Assoication of Etobicoke, the Ontrio Public School Men Teachers' Federation, and the Ontario Secondary School Teachers' Federation is offering eight-hour workshops for groups of 60 at a cost of $1500 to $2000. The teachers' dues to their federations are the main source of revenue.

The Ontario Secondary School Teachers' Federation is also funding a skills inventory and job finding technique seminar for groups of 50 teachers. The pilot project costs about $15,000. And, in early 1979, the Ottawa Board of Education sponsored a two-day seminar for those teachers expected to lose their jobs that fall.

Financing alternative education

The other principal remedy to teacher redundancy involves expanding the demand for teacher services. The market for educators can be enlarged in three main ways: through the introduction of kindergarten for four-year-olds and the extension of pre-school studies for five-year-olds in provinces where this has not yet occurred; through the improvement of special education opportunities for children who are in some way different from the typical student; and through a greater effort in educating adults.

Pre-school and special education are the responsibility of government; educators can only await initiatives in this area. And the financing of adult education depends on its venue. On-the-job training should be enlarged and paid for by the private sector, according to the Adams report. Continuing education costs are borne by the participants and by government. Any changes will have to occur at these levels. And kindergarten is largely dependent on government for its development; responsibility for its advancement would appear to lie mainly with the public sector.

* * *

Not all remedies to redundancy involve expense. The "four-five" leave plan, for example, is largely self-financing. But other remedies, including professional development, career counselling, even reassignment or dismissal, can be costly. Whose is the responsibility for meeting these costs? The answer remains unclear; and precedents in big business and government suggest current practices in education are deficient.

Examples in other sectors allocate the duty of financing a manpower plan to the initiator of that plan. Firms deciding to lay off workers often pay substantial sums in the form of severance or part-salary during the absence. Large companies reassigning employees usually finance any cost associated with the move, and both the government and private sectors are generous in their professional development spending.

School boards, however, aren't nearly as utilitarian. Severance pay is rare. Extended leave with pay is insufficient to cope with the shortages of teachers in some courses. There is a lack of correspondence between teachers' degree specialties and subjects taught, and significant numbers of teachers are without degrees. And teachers who move to find work enjoy no assistance with the costs of interviews or of the actual move.

Some boards have been accommodating to teachers, their action setting examples for other boards. The payment by one board of $250 a day for 20 days' work to a teacher to encourage him to retire early, for example, will mean $5,000 for every teacher participating in this scheme. The reasoning is that the payment will help him cope with the superannuation penalty. That same logic supports the use of financial incentives to part-time teachers or payments to redundant teachers who have been fired, but such policies are few. A resolution of the Canadian Education Association's Ottawa conference in November, calling for clarification of teacher, board, and government responsibilities in teacher retraining, points to a lack of a coherent professional development funding policy in Canadian education.

Chapter 7
Obstacles to resolving redundancy

In the wake of events of the 1970s, personal security has become supremely important. Rising tuition fees and the cost of living have spurred university graduates to seek a long-run return on their education investment. Persistent unemployment has made those with jobs more career conscious. International unrest, a slipping currency, even deterioration of the family unit, have prompted Canadians to seek stability in the last resort of self-expression and personal well-being — the work place.

This mood of retrenchment is causing teachers to move among schools or provinces less, to be less interested in alternatives to teaching, and to work until mandatory retirement. At a time when the heady expansion of the school system has halted and the supply of teachers now overshadows the demand for them, this conservative trend stands as a barrier to assuring every newly trained teacher a job.

Pensions and gratuities

Factors beyond individual preference and fear of the future are aggravating the inertia of the employed teacher force. Part-time teaching, a partial solution to redundancy and one with vast appeal to new teacher graduates hungry for classroom experience, finds limited favour among teachers nearing retirement. If they are to maximize their pension earnings, these senior teachers must also maximize their average salary over the last several years of their career. A switch to part-time employment lowers that average. The effect is more pronounced in provinces where the average is calculated over fewer rather than more years. Fewer hours of work can similarly erode one's retirement gratuity — a lump-sum payment upon retirement — by a proportion equal to the reduction in workload. The penalty can amount to thousands of dollars.

Early retirement, another anti-redundancy plan, can diminish superannuation and gratuities by an amount sufficient to deter many from leaving their jobs before their full service requirement. Quebec teachers have been able to avoid this pitfall, however, by retiring a year in advance and receiving full salary for that year.

Retraining opportunities

A scarcity of on-the-job training has, some allege, contributed to so-called burn-out of older teachers, rendering them less versatile and locking them into their current specialties. This development hampers the reassignment of teachers to subjects that are still short of staff or short of choice in the recruitment of staff; if such redeployment of teachers were easier, graduates who unfortunately hold specialties in saturated fields of education would still be able to find work. And, the quality of education, say the critics, would rise as stale educators were refreshed and younger people with new approaches were inducted into the profession.

The stress of substitute teaching

Substitute or supply teaching, a way of maintaining class continuity during teacher absences and of circulating scarce assignments among several teachers, has limitations, too. The extremely short notice given teachers for their day's work can be stressful. The money and the experience gained fall short of that enjoyed by full-time teachers. Substitute teachers often find their classes harder to control than do regular teachers because students generally have less regard for the temporary instructor. And, some teachers worry about continuity, not only of instruction, but of their own professional development;

the chance to grow with a class and see teaching effort transformed into knowledge and understanding can be stifled in supply teaching.

University policies

Despite an excess supply of teachers in some disciplines, universities continue to train and graduate students in overstaffed subjects, and some graduates continue to complain of receiving no career counselling while attending faculties of education. Some universities are changing course content in response to a changing market for teachers, but the modifications are not thorough. In some cases, the number of specialties offered students has increased, and advice is given on which specialty is marketable and which is not. But there is little known "ear-marking" of faculty of education enrolments; the choice of majors and minors still remains with the student. And universities have admitted that students continue to choose course majors and minors that bear no relation to the market realities described to them by faculty staff. Democratic though this policy may be, it is of little benefit either to teachers already employed, to school boards in search of instructors of specialty subjects such as music, art, and hard sciences, or the graduates.

Tenure and mobility

Quebec teachers and principals earn permanent positions after two years of successful teaching. Once tenured, they cannot be fired, although they can be placed on recall lists at full salary if their services are no longer required. To remain eligible for their salary, teachers may not seek alternative employment. Boards may assign such redundant teachers to a variety of tasks within the board organization, or use them as substitute teachers. But boards may not draw on unemployed teachers to ease workloads at schools — the pupil-teacher ratios must be respected. Tenure poses a costly barrier to boards hoping to ease excess supply through dismissal. The Protestant School Board of Greater Montreal, for example, placed 100 teachers on a surplus list in the 1979 school year.

Reassignment of a redundant teacher to a new school is hampered in Quebec by a limitation on the distance of the new workplace from the old. Teachers in Quebec cannot be required to take a new post more than 50 kilometres from their former job. In the face of such a policy, geographical redeployment of educators to speed the matching of supply to demand can offer only limited benefit as means of combatting redundancy.

Seniority

The insistence by unions in many provinces that dismissals due to redundancy be based on seniority, with senior teachers the least vulnerable to lay-off, also poses an obstacle to the fair reduction of the teacher force and to the maintenance of quality during a time of excess supply. Those opposing the unions say the needs of the school program should determine who should be released, and teacher ability and performance should be the criteria if further screening mechanisms are needed. This approach, it is claimed, will ensure an age balance in the teacher force with the advantages that accrue from that diversity. And, it will not unduly harm young teachers. Unions, on the other hand, consider seniority to be an unequivocal measure of an employee's importance, one which cannot be distorted or misconstrued by management, and, therefore, a measure which affords their membership the most protection.

A teacher's loss of seniority if he moves among boards also presents an obstacle to resolving redundancy, as well as to mobility generally. Transfers can be a key tool in deploying teachers efficiently, yet they can harm the experienced teacher and deter voluntary moves.

Limited alternative education

A lack of demand management policies has also obstructed the resolution of teacher redundancy. Although millions of Canadians are illiterate, and although basic education could constitute a new market of excess teachers, governments have economized in this field of instruction. Similarly, pre-school education is highly limited in some provinces and only partly developed in others, but efforts at expanding kindergarten have been slow. Special education, too, has gone hat-in-hand for some time, but although it's a priority at many school boards, it's not clear that the education of the handicapped, retarded and learning disabled enjoys a similar regard at the government level.

Rigidity of teacher timetables

Unlike many office employees, a teacher's freedom to partake of professional development is severely constrained by the demands of regular classroom schedules. On the surface, this limitation would appear to be a sound defence of limited in-service and retraining activities. However, it might be argued that planning could not only render teachers' timetables more flexible, permitting more in-service during working hours, but it could also moderate some of the disadvantages of substitute teaching. If boards planned substantial blocks of in-service sessions throughout the year, they could rely on supply teachers during the absences. Such a plan would not only permit more professional development, but would also extend work to surplus teachers and give them several weeks' notice of their substitute assignment. The advance notice would permit consultation between regular and supply teachers, and better lesson preparation.

Teacher attitudes

Teacher attitudes about their own abilities are hampering the transition of redundant teachers from the classroom to new work settings. Career counsellors working with surplus teachers in Ontario say their clients tend to underestimate their talents and feel their usefulness has ended when their contracts expire. Teachers' work habits and expectations can hinder their adjustment to a new career. They're unaccustomed to regular evaluation, harsh criticism, and assessment based on tangible output.

Preferences about job location are keeping teachers out of work and many school boards short of staff. In 1978, for example, about 300 Ontario teachers took up positions in Manitoba, responding to inter-regional discrepancies in student populations and teacher availability. There were sufficient new graduates in Winnipeg to take up some of that slack, but the postings were in rural and northern locales, unsuitable to those teachers preferring an urban setting.

* * *

Several of the barriers to a smooth matching of supply and demand for teachers are bound to be self-liquidating, either as redundancy worsens and people are forced to modify rigid views, or as the issue fades and the need for radical changes in supply or demand evaporates. Barriers of this sort include teachers' attitude toward out-of-the-way postings and for new careers, and their willingness to expand their versatility and shift among subjects.

Obstacles bound to persist as redundancy goes unabated, or to stand in the way of other advances in education independent of a mismatch of overall supply and demand, include the lesser priority accorded education in Canada, manifested in the slow growth of pre-school, adult, and special education, the training of teachers for crowded specialties, and the financial hurdles to be crossed by teachers wishing to leave teaching early or partially. These pose a long-term problem, bound to persist after redundancy has been forgotten.

Chapter 8
Summary and conclusion

A variety of factors are responsible for teacher redundancy, from declining births to the costs of education, from numbers of teachers returning to or remaining in the classroom to curriculum content. So a range of responses to the issue is warranted, some with short-term application to help ease pressing problems, others for medium- and longer-term use to set in motion forces which will eventually stabilize teacher supply and demand while ensuring students a quality education.

The short term

Certain policy shifts could occur immediately and have a pronounced effect on teacher welfare. Boards could decide to remove all deterrents to part-time teaching, to manage provincial and international exchange of teachers, and to protect the pension rights of all teachers moving among jurisdictions. Such decisions would have an immediate effect on teacher mobility and numbers of teachers in classrooms.

Boards could join with teacher federations, and perhaps with governments, to establish teacher placement agencies with a national and international referral capacity. They also might organize regular workshops for teachers facing the reality of a career shift at the close of the current term or next year.

Demand management policies with immediate impact include bringing adults into the classroom, reducing average class size and modifying teacher workloads. Teacher hours per class could be increased through introducing more options, more practical work, more individual supervision, and more remedial study.

Retraining, normally regarded as a long-term strategy, would have at least one tangible effect in the immediate-term: it would remove teachers from the classroom and open positions for those who might otherwise face unemployment.

The medium term

In the medium term, a two- or three-year span longer-range policies to influence teacher demand could begin to have an effect. Moves to expand adult education, whether of a vocational, recreational, or literacy nature, could begin. The expansion of special education for the gifted, handicapped, or retarded child could take place through steps to measure the need for this kind of education and to orient administrators and retrain teachers in the new demands this branch of education would place on them. Junior and senior kindergartens could be developed in provinces where pre-school education is minimal, and it could be expanded in the other jurisdictions. And, consideration could be given to correspondence courses as one, though limited, means of fueling the demand for teachers.

The geographic accessibility of schools, especially in rural areas, could be improved, and parents could be helped with the indirect costs of educating their youngsters, in an attempt to lower the drop-out rate. Conceivably, compulsory education could be extended, and non-teaching jobs in education could be added, with a recruitment preference given to educators.

Boards might alter teacher supply in the medium term by promoting professional development to expedite, in turn, teacher reassignment; they could encourage early retirement; and they might arrange various leaves for teachers, including plans of the four-five sort, educational leave, and leave of absence without pay.

The long term

Those policies likely to have an effect on teacher supply and demand over the long term are concentrated in education and retraining. Unversities might lessen excess supply and improve the deployment of teachers by lengthening their programs, raising their admission standards, or offering extensive career counselling to first-year students. And, retraining teachers will not only facilitate their adaption to such new endeavours as adult education and special education, but it will occupy college space with teachers already trained and help reduce the graduate output.

Policies on career counselling and retraining, for example, must follow from a coherent plan. And planning, the foundation of any forward thinking, depends on statistics on the qualifications and movement of education staff, and on their actual utilization in the school. Without adequate data on teacher stocks and flows, any attempt at planning will break down.

Some policy suggestions

Although extensive recommendations are beyond the scope of this monograph, a handful of policy options, appealing because of their authoritative endorsement, common sense, or low cost, do emerge:

1. Administrators should consider taking whatever action they can to help remove the obstacle to part-time employment and early retirement raised by superannuation and retirement gratuity regulations. Breaking down this barrier would encourage more teachers on the verge of retirement to teach part-time or, in fact, to retire, thus opening positions to younger teachers.

2. The federal government should consider the recommendations of its own commission of inquiry on educational leave that adult vocational education be expanded and that an industry levy finance this education. Expansion of this market for education manpower would create new job openings for teachers; it would also, however, boost the demand for industrial arts teachers, already in short supply, and exacerbate other shortages. The policy, therefore, must be an integral part of an overall plan.

3. Faculties of education should review their career counselling programs, and offer strong encouragement to their students to enrol in areas of education that correspond with teaching areas suffering short supply.

* * *

Whatever is done with an over-abundance of teachers will have take account of the fact that the intensity of the problem — and its priority in the minds of those who can react effectively — varies considerably among and within regions. Therefore, a range of strategies for responding to individual situations must be designed.

Bibliography

"Buy their Way out Early?" *St. Catharines Standard*, 11 April 1979.

Cairns, J.C. "Adult Functional Illiteracy in Canada." *Convergence*, vol. 10, no. 1, 1977, pp. 43-52.

Canada. Commission of Inquiry on Educational Leave and Productivity. (R.J. Adams, Chairman.) *Education and Working Canadians; Report.* Ottawa: Department of Labour, 1979.

Canadian Education Association Task Force on Public Involvement in Educational Decisions. *Results of a Gallup Poll of Public Opinion in Canada about Public Involvement in Educational Decisions.* Toronto: Canadian Education Association, 1979.

Canadian Teachers' Federation. *Canadian Teachers' Federation: Its Objectives, Its Policy, 1979-1980.* Ottawa: Canada Teachers' Federation, 1979.

_____. *Financial Implications of Declining Enrolments.* Proceedings of a seminar held in Ottawa. April 10-11, 1978. Ottawa: Canadian Teachers' Federation, 1978.

_____. *Teaching in Canada 1978.* Ottawa: Canadian Teachers' Federation, 1978.

Centre for Educational Research and Innovation. *Developments in Educational Leave of Absence.* Paris: Organisation for Economic Co-operation and Development, 1979.

Cluett, E.J., and Buffett, F., eds. *Report of the Conference on Declining Enrolments: Implications for Teacher Supply and Demand.* St. John's: Faculty of Education, Memorial University of Newfoundland, 1979.

Commission on Declining Enrolments in Ontario. (R.W.B. Jackson, Commissioner.) *Implications of Declining Enrolment for the Schools of Ontario: Implications of Declining Enrolment for the Schools of Ontario: A Statement of Effects and Solutions.* Final report. Toronto: Commission on Declining Enrolments in Ontario, 1978.

Corman, Linda, comp. *Declining Enrolments — Issues and Responses, An Annotated Bibliography.* Current Bibliography No. 11. Toronto: The Library, Reference and Information Services, Ontario Institute for Studies in Education, 1979.

Curteis, C.T. Untitled unpublished paper prepared for Canadian Education Association conference, "Creative Uses of Human Resources: Retraining — Can it Help?" (Ottawa, November 22-24, 1979).

Davie, Lynn, et al. *Educational Needs and Learning Conditions of Adult Learners.* Working Paper No. 17. Toronto: Commission on Declining Enrolments in Ontario, 1978.

Dewey, Martin. "Teachers Learn How to Get, Fit Into New Jobs." *Toronto Globe and Mail*, 11 June 1979, Report on Business.

Draper, James, and Keating, Donald. *Instructors of Adults*. Working Paper No. 18. Toronto: Commission on Declining Enrolments in Ontario, 1978.

Due, John F. *Government Finance: Economics of the Public Sector*. Nobleton, Ontario: Irwin-Dorsey Ltd., 1968.

Economic Council of Canada. *Eighth Annual Review: Design for Decision-Making — An Application to Human Resources Policies*. Ottawa: Information Canada, 1971.

Ellmen, Eugene. "Teachers Urged to Take Time Off." *St. Catharines (Ont.) Standard*, 6 June 1979.

Enns, Robin J. et al. *The Effect of Declining Enrolment on School Objectives and Programs*. Working Paper No. 31. Toronto: Commission on Declining Enrolments in Ontario, 1979.

Fiaz, Nelly. *Teacher In-Service Training: A Luxury or a Tool of Survival? The Problem of Continuing Teacher Education as it Appears in the Briefs Submitted to the Commission on Declining Enrolments in Ontario, 1978*. Information Bulletin No. 16. Toronto: Commission on Declining Enrolments in Ontario, 1978.

Fox, Marcel R. "Positive Strategies for Retraining." Unpublished paper presented to the Canadian Education Association seminar, "Creative Uses of Human Resources: Retraining — Can it Help?" (Ottawa, November 22-24, 1979).

Friedman, Milton. *Capitalism and Freedom*. Chicago: University of Chicago Press, 1962.

Girhiny, John. *Professional Development and Declining Enrolments in Ontario*. Information Bulletin No. 8. Toronto: Commission on Declining Enrolments in Ontario, 1978.

Hainsworth, Mary. *Report on Second and Third Languages*. Working Paper No. 37. Toronto: Commission on Declining Enrolments in Ontario, 1978.

Hughes, A.S., et al. *Actual and Projected Effects of Declining Enrolments upon School Program Offerings*. Working Paper No. 20. Toronto: Commission on Declining Enrolments in Ontario, 1978.

Hunt, David E., and Hunt, Janice S. *On the Psychology of Declining Enrolment: With a Brief Review of Attempts to Cushion the Negative Effects of Professional Unemployment*. Working Paper No. 12. Toronto: Commission on Declining Enrolments in Ontario, 1978.

Jackson, R.W.B. *Implications for Education of Recent Trends in Live Births and International and Interprovincial Migration of Children*. Toronto: Canadian Education Association, 1977.

Kervin, John B. *Declining Enrolments and Teacher-Board Negotiations: Bargaining Conditions of Employment*. Working Paper No. 6. Toronto: Commission on Declining Enrolments in Ontario, 1978.

Kobrick, Judi B., and Reich, Carol. *Declining Enrolments and its Ramifications for Special Education*. Working Paper No. 36. Toronto: Commission on Declining Enrolments in Ontario, 1978.

Kumar, Krishna. *Job Sharing Through Part-Time Contracts, A Consideration in the Context of Declining School Enrolments in Ontario.* Working Paper No. 39. Toronto: Commission on Declining Enrolments in Ontario, 1978.

Lakehead Board of Education Task Force on Declining Enrolment, Subcommittee on Part-Time Teaching. *Part-Time Teaching: A Consideration in an Era of Declining Enrolment.* Thunder Bay: Lakehead Board of Education, 1979.

Leithwood, K., and Montgomery, D. *Effects of Declining Enrolments on the Curriculum: Perceptions of Supervisory Officers.* Working Paper No. 29. Toronto: Commission on Declining Enrolments in Ontario. 1978.

Lipovenko, Dorothy. "Teachers Tempted with Early Retirement." *Toronto Globe and Mail,* 8 February 1978.

Manitoba Department of Education Research Branch. "Teacher Demand/Supply Manpower Outlook in Manitoba." Unpublished paper. Winnipeg: Research Branch, Manitoba Department of Education, 8 May 1979.

Manitoba Teachers' Society Task Force on Declining Enrolments. *Report.* Winnipeg: Manitoba Teachers' Society, 1975.

McCallum, Peggy. "Workshops Help 60 Laid-off Teachers to Rebuild Shattered Self-Confidence." *Toronto Globe and Mail,* 10 June 1978.

Moir, Carmen F. "Professional Development and Inner City Problems." *Education Canada,* December 1974, pp. 20-21.

Newfoundland Task Force on Education. *Perspectives on Declining Enrolments in the Schools of Newfoundland and Labrador.* Interim Report. St. John's: Newfoundland Department of Education, 1978.

"OTF to Explore Placing Teachers Abroad." *OTF/FEO Interaction,* October 1979.

Ontario Public School Men Teachers' Federation. *Brief to the Commission on Declining Enrolments.* Toronto: Ontario Public School Men Teachers' Federation, 1978.

Organisation for Economic Co-operation and Development. *Teacher Policies in a New Context.* Paris: Organisation for Economic Co-operation and Development, 1979.

Padro, Susan. *Survey of Staff Development and Curriculum Services for Quality Education.* Working Paper No. 8. Toronto: Commission on Declining Enrolments in Ontario, 1978.

"Part Time Teaching — A Growing Factor at Work." *BCTF Newsletter,* 17 November 1977.

Phillips, Iris. "Enrollment Problems Worry School Units." *Charlottetown Guardian,* 27 April 1979.

Price, John T., and Cash, Larry M. *Teachers Without Classrooms: A Career Planning Guide for Teachers Leaving the Profession.* Toronto: Guidance Centre, Faculty of Education, University of Toronto, 1979.

"Province has to 'Import' Teachers." *Winnipeg Free Press*, 20 April 1979.

Regan, Ellen M. *Early Childhood Care and Education*. Working Paper No. 28. Toronto: Commission on Declining Enrolments in Ontario, 1978.

Rideout, Brock E., et. al. *Educational, Social, and Financial Implications to School Boards of Declining Enrolments*. Toronto: Ontario Ministry of Education, 1977.

Samuelson, Paul A., and Scott, Anthony. *Economics*. Toronto: McGraw-Hill, 1966.

Schwartz, Arthur M., and McGowan, Patrick. *Declining Enrolment: Implications for British Columbia's Public School System*. Vancouver: Educational Research Institute of British Columbia, 1977.

Shallow, William. "Life Long Learning: Are We Making Any Progress?" *Education Canada*, Spring 1979, pp. 43-45.

Smith, Dorothy, E., et al. *Working Paper on the Implications of Declining Enrolment for Women Teachers in Public Elementary and Secondary Schools in Ontario*. Working Paper No. 24. Toronto: Commission on Declining Enrolments in Ontario, 1978.

Statistics Canada. *Elementary and Secondary School Enrolments 1977-78*. Cat. No. 81-210. Ottawa: Statistics Canada, 1979.

_____. *1976 Census of Population and Housing*. Cat. No. 92-832. Ottawa: Statistics Canada, 1976.

_____. *Salaries and Qualifications of Teachers in Public Elementary and Secondary Schools*. Annual. Cat. No. 81-202. Ottawa: Statistics Canada, 1961 to 1978.

Sullivan, Keith. *Community Schools: A Solution to Declining Enrolment*. Working Paper No. 3. Toronto: Commission on Declining Enrolments in Ontario, 1978.

Thomas, A.M. *Adult Basic Education and Literacy Activities in Canada, 1975-76*. Toronto: World Literacy of Canada, 1976.

Toronto Board of Education. Unpublished untitled report from the Director of Education to the Chairman and members of the Board of Education. Toronto, 18 November, 1977, p. 17.

Unesco. *Readings in the Economics of Education*. Paris: Unesco, 1968.

Warren, Philip J. *A Study of Unemployed Teachers*. St. John's: Institute for Educational Research and Development, Memorial University of Newfoundland, 1979.

Williams. Peter. *Planning Teacher Demand and Supply*. Paris: Internatioⁱal Institute for Educational Planning, Unesco, 1979.

Yakimishyn, M.P. "An Aging Teaching Force: Some Implications." Unpublished paper. Winnipeg: Manitoba Department of Education, 1978.

"Year-off-without-pay Plan Worries Teacher Group." *Vancouver Sun*, 10 September 1979.